About the Author

Our founder and C.E.O, Carlton Reed, CPhT. became a Certified Pharmacy Technician in 2014, beginning his career at CVS Pharmacy. He is the author of several books including "PTCE Notes" both first and second edition, which has helped students across the United States become nationally Certified Pharmacy Technicians.

For nearly 5 years, Carlton has help dedicated students launch their careers in the pharmacy industry.

Disclaimer

This book is intended to be used as a study guide and does not guarantee successful completion of any pharmacy technician certification examination. This guide is designed to assist with exam preparation and is not intended to replace other study materials or academic texts. The practice tests are the opinions of the author and have not been tested, reviewed or endorsed by any organization.

While every attempt has been made to include accurate and up-to-date information, it is possible changes and amendments have been made since publication.

This book is not to be used as a reference for patient care.

Publishing

© Rx Health Academy LLC. All rights reserved. No part of this publication may be reproduced or distributed in any form or by any means, electronic or otherwise, without written permission from Rx Health Academy LLC.

This book was written by Carlton Reed, CPhT. and edited by Erin J. Marts, B.S., CHES.

Dedication

To Rx Health Academy's Students and Allum.

Table of Contents

Introduction — Pg. 5

Pharmacology for Pharmacy Technicians — Pg. 9
  1.1 Names of Pharmaceuticals
  1.2 Therapeutic Equivalence, Drug Interactions, and Relevance To Patient Medical History
  1.3 Types of Interactions
  1.4 Pharmaceutical Characteristics
  1.5 Drug Administration and Duration of Therapy
  1.6 Common Unwanted Drug Effects
  1.7 Drug Classifications

Pharmacy Law and Regulations — Pg. 33
  2.1 Routine Practices With Hazardous Substances And Waste
  2.2 Controlled Substance Documentation
  2.3 Professional Standards
  2.4 FDA Recall Classification
  2.5 Pharmacy Personnel Roles
  2.6 Facility Requirements
  2.7 Reference Materials

Sterile and Non-Sterile Compounding — Pg. 59
  3.1 Infection Control for Compounding
  3.2 Documentation
  3.3 Product Stability
  3.4 Equipment and Supplies
  3.5 Compounding Risk

Medication Safety — Pg. 73
  4.1 Medication Errors and Error Prevention
  4.2 Information for the Patient
  4.3 Specific Recommendations
  4.4 Similar Medications
  4.5 Common Safety Strategies

Pharmacy Quality Assurance — Pg. 87
  5.1 Quality Assurance Practices
  5.2 Education Standards and Information Technology
  5.3 Infection Control for Quality Assurance

Pharmacy Math — Pg. 97
  6.1 Calculating Day's Supply
  6.2 IV Calculations
  6.3 Measurement Conversions
  6.4 Roman Numerals
  6.5 Alligation

Medication Order Entry and Fill Process — Pg. 107
  7.1 Order Entry Process
  7.2 Fill Process
  7.3 Labeling
  7.4 Packaging and Dispensing Process

Pharmacy Inventory Management — Pg. 119
  8.1 Using Numerical Information
  8.2 Product Lists
  8.3 Ordering and Receiving

Pharmacy Billing and Reimbursement — Pg. 129
  9.1 Obtaining Patient Insurance Information
  9.2 Key Terms
  9.3 Types of Insurance Coverage
  9.4 Managed Care Programs

Pharmacy Information Systems and Usage Applications — Pg. 147
  10.1 Computer Applications for Use When Dispensing Prescriptions
  10.2 Computer Applications
  10.3 Reports
  10.4 Standards of Electronic Health Records

Introduction

A pharmacy technician is a health care provider who performs, pharmacy-related functions, generally working under the direct supervision of a licensed pharmacist. In this career, you work alongside pharmacists and pharmacy aides to help customers, complete administrative duties and handle medication prescriptions.

Your main duty will be filling prescriptions. Due to the sensitive nature of medication, a big part of your job is to verify that the prescription information is accurate. You might work in a variety of pharmacy environments, such as a retail setting, hospital, insurance, IV lab or mail-order pharmaceuticals companies.

Key Terms

- → *Certification* is the process of granting recognition to an individual who has met predetermined qualifications.
- → The *Certified Pharmacy Technician (CPhT)* designation is given to an individual with the knowledge, skill, and ability necessary to function as a pharmacy technician.
- → An individual who passes the *Pharmacy Technician Certification Exam (PTCE)* exam earns the creditail CPhT.
    - ◆ **Example:** John L. Doe, CPhT.

The *Pharmacy Technician Certification Board*, also known as the PTCB is a non-governmental agency that administers the Pharmacy Technician Certification Exam. The exam is broken down into nine domains; in-other-words the exam is testing your knowledge in nine different subjects. This study guide will provide you with a comprehensive review of all the concepts tested on the PTCE. Each chapter focuses on one of the nine domain areas and contains 10 review questions and answer explanations.

By the end of this book you will be fully prepared for your Pharmacy Technician Certification Exam. Once passing the PTCE you will be eligible to license as a Pharmacy Tech in your state.

Let's get started!

About the Pharmacy Technician Certification Exam

The **Pharmacy Technician Certification Board** is responsible for ensuring that Pharmacy technicians meet predetermined standards that convey competency in the field of Pharmacy. These standards include having Knowledge and Skills pertaining to Pharmacy practice. In order to become a Certified Pharmacy Technician interested candidates need to apply for certification through the PTCB website, www.ptcb.org. In order to qualify for certification candidates must meet the following criteria

Educational Requirements for Pharmacy Technicians
- ❏ High School Diploma or an equivalent educational diploma
- ❏ Provide full disclosure of all criminal actions and all State Board of Pharmacy registration or licensure action
- ❏ Receive a passing score on the Pharmacy Technician Certification Exam (PTCE)

The **pharmacy technician certification exam** is a computer-based 90 question multiple choice examination given over a two-hour time frame of that time 1 hour and 50 minutes are allotted to the actual test the remaining 2 minutes are for a tutorial and a post exam survey 80 out of 90 questions or scored and 10 questions are unscored test takers will not be able to determine the differences between the scored and unscored questions because the unscored questions are randomly distributed throughout the exam.

The PTCB uses a scaled scoring system. Candidates receive scores ranging from 1,000 to 1,600 a passing grade is a 1400. As per the Pharmacy Technician Certification Board test questions are determined based on 9 knowledge domains. These domains can be seen on the next page.

Scheduling Your Exam.

The PTCB is Administered at Pearson VUE testing centers. Pearson VUE testing centers are available Nationwide. They offer computer-based testing for a multitude of professions including the Pharmacy Technician Certification Exam potential CPhT candidates can sign up for testing slots by following these directions:

1. Go to *www.PTCB.org*
2. Click on "apply for certification"
3. Create an account or log on to an existing account
4. Pay the $129 fee
5. Receive authorization to schedule and take the PTCE. Candidates are sent an authorization to test letter via email
6. Go to www.pearsonvue.com/ptcb/ or call 866-902-0593 to schedule an appointment
7. Choose a date, time, and location that works best for you to take your exam

Unofficial preliminary results are available immediately after taking the exam. Official exam results are scored and will be posted to your account within 2 to 3 weeks.

Pharmacy Technician Certification Exam (PTCE) Blueprint

Knowledge Domain and Areas	% of PTCE
Pharmacology for Pharmacy Technicians	13.75%
Pharmacy Law and Regulations	12.50%
Sterile and Non-Sterile Compounding	8.75%
Medication Safety	12.50%
Pharmacy Quality Assurance	7.50%
Medication Order Entry and Fill Process	17.50%
Pharmacy Inventory Management	8.75%
Pharmacy Billing and Reimbursement	8.75%
Pharmacy Information System Usage and Application	10%

This book covers the nine content areas listed in the official PTCE Blueprint. As you study for the exam be mindful to play to your strengths; however, be careful not to ignore the smaller knowledge domains. Every point counts !

Chapter 1

Pharmacology for Pharmacy Technicians

Rx Health Academy

General Information

Questions concerning pharmacology will occupy nearly 14% of the Pharmacy Technician Certification Board (PTCB) exam. You'll need to know all about drugs, their interactions and side-effects, as well as common dosages. Be sure to seek additional information about concepts that give you trouble.

What you'll learn in this chapter

- Generic and brand names of pharmaceuticals
- Therapeutic equivalence
- Drug interactions
- Strengths/dose, dosage forms, physical appearance, routes of administration, and duration of drug therapy
- Common and severe side or adverse effects, allergies, and therapeutic contraindications associated with medications
- Dosage and indication of legend, OTC medications, herbal and dietary supplements

Chapter Outline

1.1 Names of Pharmaceuticals
1.2 Therapeutic Equivalence, Drug Interactions, and Relevance To Patient Medical History
1.3 Types of Interactions
1.4 Pharmaceutical Characteristics
1.5 Drug Administration and Duration of Therapy
1.6 Common Unwanted Drug Effects
1.7 Drug Classifications

Chapter 1: *Pharmacology for Pharmacy Technician*

Chapter 1: *Pharmacology for Pharmacy Technician*

1.1 NAMES OF PHARMACEUTICALS

Like in any other profession, knowing and using the appropriate vocabulary is an important part of the job. Being familiar with common pharmaceutical names and spellings will make it easier to understand patients and communicate with other healthcare professionals. In the realm of pharmacy, it is crucial to be exact with names and spelling, since two medications may have very similar names but be used for vastly different purposes

Brand Names

Brand names are typically shorter than generic names; therefore, drug manufacturers often use brand names to advertise new drugs. It is important to note:

- One generic drug may have multiple brand names, depending on drug formulation and manufacturer
    - (e.g., zolpidem is found in Ambien, Edluar, Inter-mezzo, and Zolpimist).
- The first letter of a brand name should be <u>capitalized</u>, as it is patented by the drug manufacturer.

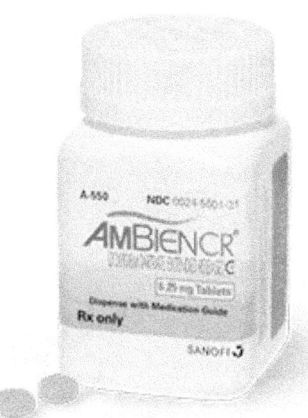

Figure 1.1.a

Generic Names

Generic drugs are lower-cost versions of brand name drugs. Pharmaceuticals are classified into drug classes based on how they work.

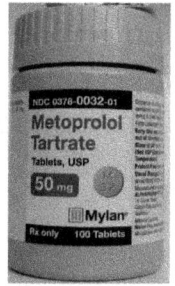

Figure 1.1.b

- Oftentimes, the suffix of a drug's generic name indicates its drug class.
    - For example, pharmaceuticals that end with -olol (e.g., metoprolol and pro-pra-nolol)

Are blood-pressure lowering agents known as *beta blockers*.

OTC Medications

Over-the-counter (OTC) drugs are simply those that can be bought without a prescription. The U.S. Food and Drug Administration (FDA) has deemed them safe and effective when patients follow the directions on the label and as directed by a healthcare professional.

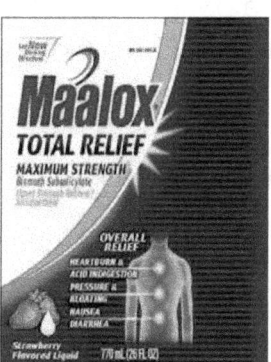

Figure 1.1.c

Herbal and Dietary Supplements

Herbal and dietary supplements can often be purchased without a prescription, but they are regulated differently than OTC drugs by the U.S. Food and Drug Administration.

Figure 1.1.d

Vitamins, minerals, and herbs are all considered *"dietary supplements"* because they contain "dietary ingredients" meant to add nutritional value to one's diet. It is important to:

1. ask patients specifically if they are taking any dietary supplements
2. Offer examples such as (B 12, garlic, ginkgo biloba, ginseng, and St. John's Wort) can help trigger a patient's memory.

1.2 RELATION OF THERAPEUTIC EQUIVALENCE AND DRUG INTERACTIONS TO PATIENT MEDICAL HISTORY

Pharmaceutical drug variations, alternatives, and equivalents are essential to remember. Their relation to drug interactions play a large role in how it affects a patient. Referring to a patient's medical history will be a high priority in the success of drug therapy.

Therapeutic Equivalence

Therapeutic equivalence is designated when two drug products meet strict criteria in accordance with the Food and Drug Administration (FDA) Orange Book.

- Pharmaceutical equivalents,
- pharmaceutical alternatives,
- and therapeutic equivalents all fall under the umbrella of therapeutic equivalence.

Figure 1.2.a

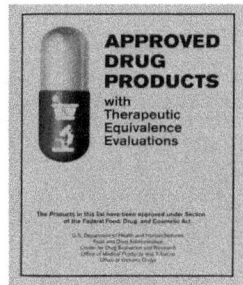

Drug Interactions

Drug interactions occur for many reasons and can range in severity from mild to life-threatening. It is important to educate patients about the potential for drug interactions to occur and to describe any adverse reactions they may experience.

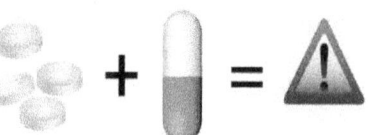

Figure 1.2.b

Patient's Medical History

Obtaining an accurate and complete *medical history* of a patient is necessary for understanding how best to care for that individual. Having a complete understanding of a patient's allergies, medical problems, and medication history helps healthcare professionals select the most beneficial pharmaceuticals for a patient while avoiding potential interactions.

Figure 1.2.c

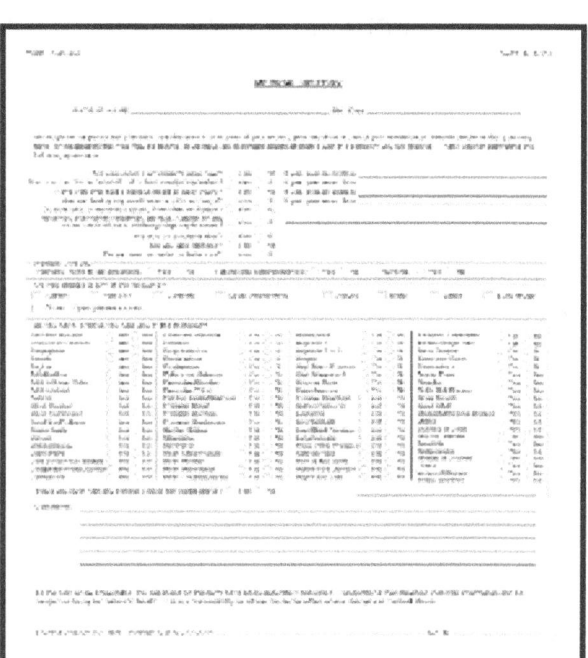

1.3 TYPES OF INTERACTIONS

Drugs can interact with other drugs, diseases, and even laboratory results. Common interactions will vary depending on the practice setting (e.g., community and hospital). It is important to remember that individual responses to interactions will vary.

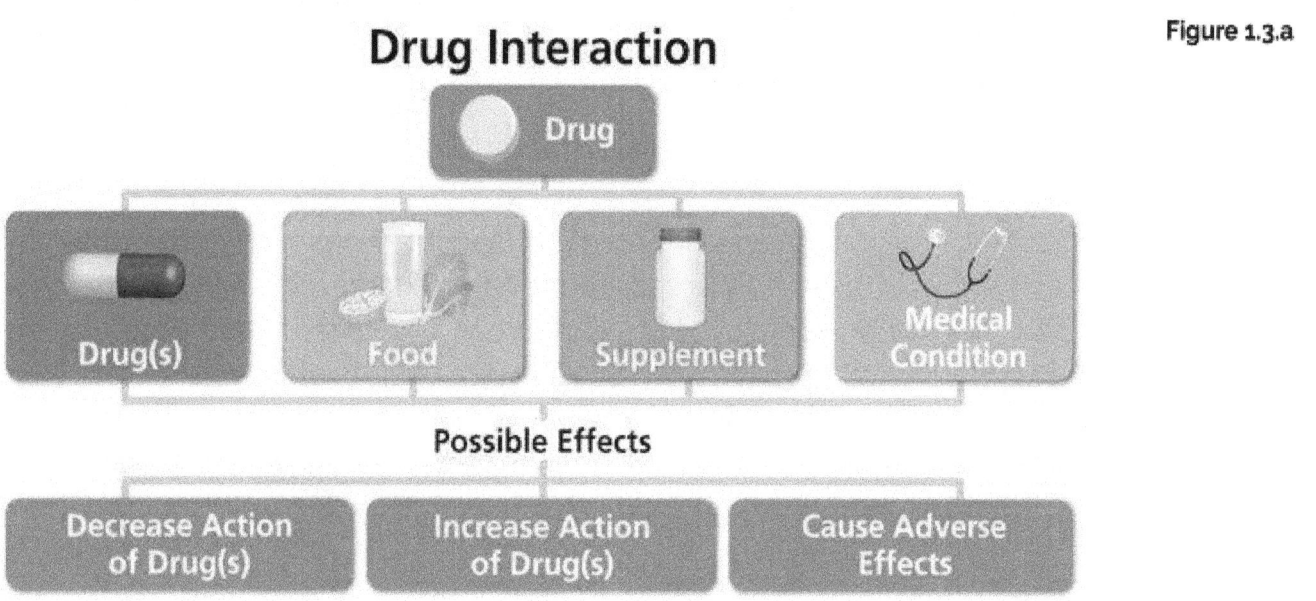

Figure 1.3.a

1. Drug-Disease

Drugs that are used for more than one disease may worsen another disease. For example, using ibuprofen for pain in a patient with heart failure is a potential *drug-disease interaction*, as ibuprofen can cause fluid retention and worsen heart failure. If a patient with heart failure tolerates ibuprofen well, then the interaction is not clinically significant; however, if the patient's heart failure worsens after starting ibuprofen, then a new approach to managing pain should be considered.

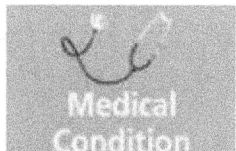

Figure 1.3.b

2. Drug-Drug

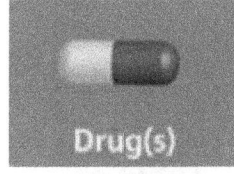

Figure 1.3.c

Interactions between two (or more) prescription drugs are common, can occur for a variety of reasons, and should be evaluated prior to drug dispensing. Taking multiple medications, being prescribed drugs by multiple healthcare professionals, and using multiple pharmacies can increase a patient's risk of experiencing a *drug-drug interaction*.

3. Drug-OTC

OTC drugs can interact with other OTC drugs or prescription drugs; however, patients can purchase OTC drugs without first talking to their physician, pharmacist, or other healthcare professional, so they may not be aware of potential ***drug-OTC interactions***. For example, if a patient is prescribed an acetaminophen-containing drug [e.g., oxycodone/acetaminophen (Percocet)] then also purchases OTC acetaminophen (the active ingredient in Tylenol), there is an increased risk of serious liver damage.

4. Drug-Dietary Supplement

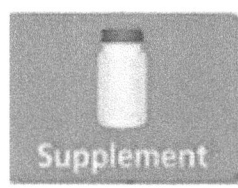

Figure 1.3.e

St. John's Wort has the most potential for interactions with prescription drugs. For example, it has been associated with an increased risk of bleeding with blood-thinning prescription drug warfarin and enhanced effect of prescription drugs used for depression and anxiety. Similarly, Vitamin E at high doses has been associated with an increased risk of bleeding; combining Vitamin E with warfarin further increases this risk for a ***drug-dietary supplement interaction***.

5. Drug-Laboratory

Laboratory test results are rarely affected by medications; however, because test results may be falsely positive or negative, it is important to be aware of the potential for a ***drug-laboratory interaction*** to occur. For example, finasteride (used to shrink an enlarged prostate) may reduce a man's prostate-specific antigen (PSA), a laboratory test used to screen for prostate cancer). If laboratory results are interpreted without knowledge of the patient taking finasteride (and therefore having a falsely low PSA), it could interfere with the timely diagnosis of prostate cancer.

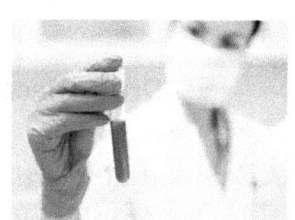

Figure 1.3.f

6. Drug-Nutrient

Figure 1.3.g

Nutrients include vitamin supplements and nutrients from food. Calcium is an essential nutrient that can be ingested in the form of food (milk), dietary supplement (calcium supplements), or OTC drug (antacid). In any form, taking calcium at the same time as a fluoroquinolone antibiotics [e.g., ciprofloxacin (Cipro)] has the potential to decrease absorption of the antibiotic in the body, thereby decreasing the ability of the antibiotic to fight infection, causing ***drug-nutrient interactions***.

1.4 PHARMACEUTICAL CHARACTERISTICS

It is important for pharmacy technicians to be familiar with the physical appearance, common dosages, dosage forms, and strengths of all pharmaceuticals. This will make it easier to identify the correct drug, communicate with other healthcare professionals, and even detect potential fake prescriptions. Questions on the PTCB Exam on this topic may include calculations.

Physical Appearance

A drug's size, shape, color, and dosage form make up its *physical appearance*. The physical appearance of a drug may differ between manufacturers, and especially between brand and generic drug manufacturers; as such, if a patient reports that the color of their tablet has changed from last month to this month, then it may not mean that the wrong drug was given. In the case of warfarin, however, each of the nine tablet strengths is a different color, which helps patients (and healthcare professionals) identify that they are taking the correct one.

Strength

Drug *strength* is the amount of active drug in any given dosage form. The drug strength will be noted immediately after a drug name and is commonly expressed in terms of milligrams (mg) or micrograms (mcg) for oral tablets or capsules, milligrams/milliliter (mg/mL) for liquid preparations, and grams (g) for topical creams, gels, and ointments. Drugs may also be available in more than one strength. For example, tablets of the blood-thinning drug warfarin are available as 1 mg, 2 mg, 2.5 mg, 3 mg, 4 mg, 5 mg, 6 mg, 7.5 mg, and 10 mg.

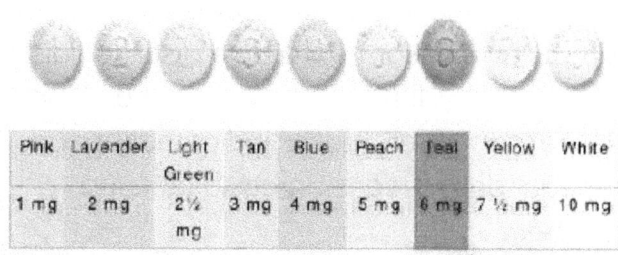

Pink	Lavender	Light Green	Tan	Blue	Peach	Teal	Yellow	White
1 mg	2 mg	2½ mg	3 mg	4 mg	5 mg	6 mg	7½ mg	10 mg

Figure 1.4.a

Dose

The *dose* of a drug is the amount to be taken at any one time and is determined by a variety of patient-specific factors, such as age, weight, kidney function, and other diagnoses and drugs. In the case of warfarin, a patient may be prescribed warfarin 8 mg once daily. In that case, the dose is 8 mg, but two warfarin tablets of the 4 mg strength are needed to achieve the target dose. In some cases, the total daily or weekly dose is provided (e.g., "Take alendronate 70 mg by mouth once weekly") or the dose may be less, well, prescriptive (e.g., "Apply a small amount of cream twice a day to the affected arm").

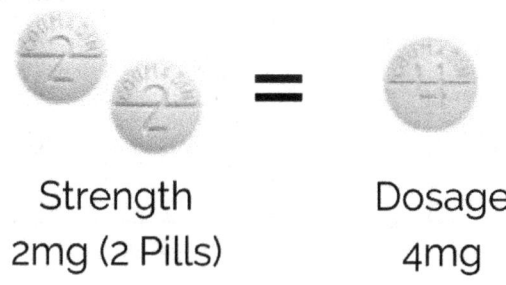

Strength
2mg (2 Pills)

Dosage
4mg

Figure 1.4.b

Dosage and Indication of Legend

The *indication of legend* is the reason for which a prescription or OTC drug is prescribed or recommended. In keeping with the drug's FDA approval (or) the dosage for a drug may differ by indication. For example, the starting dose of sertraline (Zoloft) for post-traumatic stress disorder is 25 mg once daily, but for major depressive disorder it is 50 mg once daily. Finally, if a drug is prescribed for a reason other than its indicated legend, then that drug is considered to be used *"off-label"*.

Dosage Forms

A drug's ***dosage form*** is another term for its physical form. Drugs come in all shapes (e.g., tablets, capsules, solutions, creams, and patches) and sizes (e.g., 25 mcg, 500 mg, and 1 g). One important dosage form to counsel on is the ***suspension***, as it needs to be shaken in order to evenly disperse the suspended particles and deliver a uniform dose to the patient.

Common Dosage Forms

Solid	Liquid	Semi-solid	Suppository	Aerosol	Transdermal
• Tablets • Capsules • Powders	• Syrups • Elixirs • Spirits • IV Meds	• Creams • Ointment • Gels	• Rectum • Vagina • Urethra	• Inhalers	• Patches

Table 1.4.a

1.5 DRUG ADMINISTRATION AND DURATION OF THERAPY

Indicating routes of administration, and adhering to the scripted duration of a regimen are two key components to a successful drug therapy. It is important to be familiar with all common routes of administration for each pharmaceutical, as well as how long drug therapy will be used to treat a patient.

Administration Routes

Common ***administration routes*** include inhalation, oral, nasal, rectal, vaginal, topical, and transdermal. It is of the utmost importance to accurately identify the intended way for a drug to be given. In the case that a patient would take a capsule by mouth instead of inserting it into the rectum, drug absorption, safety, and/or efficacy may be compromised. If there is a question about the route of administration, then a call to the prescriber should be placed to clarify.

Duration of Drug Therapy

The ***duration of drug therapy*** is determined by the diagnosis and other patient-specific factors. Chronic conditions, like depression or diabetes, may require ongoing medication treatment. More acute problems, like pain or an infection, may just need to be treated for a few days or weeks. If patients take medication for less or more time than intended, it could cause problems down the road, such as uncontrolled diabetes or antibiotic resistance.

1.6 COMMON UNWANTED DRUG EFFECTS

Unwanted adverse (negative) drug side effects are common and can range from mild to severe reactions. Patient counseling should include education about what side effects to look out for and what to do in the case that side effects occur.

Common Side Effects

Side effects for a given drug can often be predicted based on how a drug works; however, since **side effects** are not part of the intended therapeutic effects of a drug, they are considered unwanted. Common side effects may include headache, stomach upset, or dizziness; some side effects go away over time while others are expected to continue for as long as a drug is being used. Even with the same drug, side effects may also differ by dose, dosage form, and route of administration.

Severe Side Effects

Severe side effects are those that negatively impact a person's wellbeing or their disease management. Muscle pain and cramping are common side effects of -statin medications used for high cholesterol. Over time and with dose increases, the muscle pain may be unbearable and cause the patient to stop taking his or her medication. On the other hand, a patient may not feel any different on their -statin medication, but a laboratory test may show that they have developed liver dysfunction. This would be another severe side effect, though not one that makes the patient feel differently.

Allergies

While a drug's most common side effects can often be predicted, **allergies** are much less predictable because the body's immune response differs significantly from person to person. Allergic reactions account for just 10% of all drug side effects; however, allergic reactions can be life-threatening. **Anaphylaxis** is the most serious allergic reaction and can result in hives, swelling of the face or throat, wheezing, and even death; antibiotics are the most common cause of anaphylactic reactions. It is important to note that some patients are allergic to inactive (non-drug) ingredients, such as gluten or dye; drug compounding allows for medications to be made to suit specific patient needs such as these.

Therapeutic Contraindications

"Therapeutic contraindication" is another term for a case in which two drugs should not be used together. Generally speaking, the potential risks outweigh the potential benefits. A *"relative contraindication"* suggests that caution should be used when combining two drugs, whereas two drugs that are identified as an *"absolute contraindication"* should never be used together because of the potential for a life-threatening situation to occur. Drugs may also be contra-indicated in certain conditions like pregnancy or because of age.

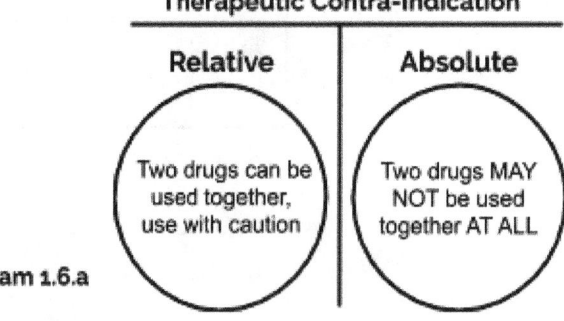

Diagram 1.6.a

1.7 DRUG CLASSIFICATIONS

Pharmacology has two major branches:

- **Pharmacokinetics**, which refers to the absorption, distribution, metabolism, and excretion of drugs
- **Pharmacodynamics**, which refers to the molecular, biochemical, and physiological effects of drugs, including drug mechanism of action.

Drugs are grouped by their common actions and effects on the body, this grouping is called a **drug classification**. Knowing the **stem** or root word of a medication will help you identify a drug. Some drugs within the same classification (class) may also be apart of a **sub-group** based on it's formulary classification as well. Let's take a look at some common drug classifications and their stems below.

Anti-anxiety, Antiepileptic, Antidepressant and Sedative Agents

An **anxiolytic** is the medication or other intervention that inhibits anxiety. This effect is in contrast to anxiogenic agents, which increase anxiety. Anticonvulsants are a diverse group of pharmacological agents used in the treatment of epileptic seizures.

Antidepressants are drugs used for the treatment of major depressive disorder and other conditions, including dysthymia, anxiety disorders, obsessive–compulsive disorder, eating disorders, etc. Doses of sedatives such as benzodiazepines when used as a hypnotic to induce sleep tend to be higher than the amounts used to relieve anxiety; whereas only low doses are needed to provide a peaceful effect.

You should familiarize yourself with the stems of Anti-anxiety, Antiepileptic, Antidepressant and Sedative Agents below.

Stems of Anti-anxiety, Antiepileptic, Antidepressant and Sedative Agents

Stem	Sub - Group	Drug Example
-azepam	Benzodiazepine anxiolytic	temazepam
-pidem	Zolpidem-type of Sedative hypnotic	zolpidem
-plon	Non-benzodiazepine anxiolytic	zaleplon

Chart 1.7.a

Chapter 1: *Pharmacology for Pharmacy Technician*

Anti-infectives

Anti-infectives is a general term used to describe any medicine that is capable of inhibiting the spread of an infectious organism or by killing the infectious organism outright. This term encompasses all of the following categories:

- Antibiotics
- Antifungals
- Anthelmintics
- Antimalarials
- Antiprotozoals
- Antituberculosis agents
- Antivirals

Refer to the table of stems for Anti-infective Agents that you should know.

Anti-infective Agents

Stem	Description	Example
-bactam	Beta-lactamase	sulbactam
cef-	Cephalosporins	cefepime
-cillin	Penicillins	piperacillin
-conazole	Miconazole- type antifungal	Itraconazole
-cycline	Tetracycline	Doxycycline
-ezolid	Oxazolidone	Linezolid
-oxacin	Quinoines	Levofloxacin
-vir	Antiviral	Acyclovir

Chart 1.7.b

Antiviral agents

Although Antiviral agents are apart of the Anti-infectives group they have some unique characteristics worth mentioning. ***Antiviral*** agents are used to inhibit production of viruses that cause disease. Most antiviral agents are only effective while the virus is replicating. ***Antiretroviral*** drugs inhibit the reproduction of retroviruses—viruses composed of RNA rather than DNA.

Types of Antiviral agents

- adamantane antivirals
- antiviral boosters
- antiviral combinations
- antiviral interferons
- chemokine receptor antagonist
- integrase strand transfer inhibitor
- miscellaneous antivirals
- neuraminidase inhibitors
- NNRTIs
- NS5A inhibitors

Cardiovascular Agents

Cardiovascular agents are medicines that are used to treat medical conditions associated with the heart or the circulatory system (blood vessels), such as arrhythmias, blood clots, coronary artery disease, high or low blood pressure, high cholesterol, heart failure, and stroke.

There are many different classes of drugs that fall under the general term cardiovascular agent. Some work directly on the blood vessels surrounding the heart, reducing how much force the heart has to pump against.

Others lower cholesterol levels and help reduce the formation of atherosclerotic plaques which cause blood vessel narrowing. Some work in the kidneys to increase fluid and salt loss or improve blood flow through the kidneys. The type of cardiovascular disease the person has determines which class of cardiovascular agent to use.

Cardiovascular Agent Stems — Chart 1.7.c

Stem	Description	Drug Example
-arone	Antiarrhythmics	Amiodarone
-azosin	Prazosin	Terazosin
-dralazine	Hydrazine-phthalazine	Hydralazine
-olol	Beta blockers	Metoprolol
-pril	ACE Inhibitor	Lisinopril
-sartan	Angiotensin II receptor	Losartan
-taplase	Plasminogen activator	Reteplase
-vastatin	HMG- CoA reductase	Simvastatin

Dermatological Agents

Topical dermatological agents are applied directly on the skin to treat skin conditions. They may deliver medicines to prevent or treat skin disorders or have inert creams and ointments for routine skin care to maintain the skin, which may be susceptible to skin disorders.

Topical dermatological agents include local anesthetics, cleansing agents, anti-inflammatory agents, anti-infective agents, emollients, astringents, agents to treat acne, antivirals, antifungals, agents for psoriasis such as topical corticosteroids, and so on. Many of these medications are available over the counter in low strengthens such as Hydrocortisone. However some medications such as Acyclovir are available only with a prescription.

Stems for Dermatological Agents

Stem	Description	Drug Example
-cort	Cortisone derivative	Hydrocortisone
-olone	Steroids	Triamcinolone
-onide	Steroids	Fluocinonide
Sulfa	Antimicrobial	Silver Sulfadiazine
-vir	Antiviral	Acyclovir

Chart 1.7.d

Ears, Eyes, Nose and Throat Agents

Medications in this category treat a variety of conditions and are sometimes referred to as medications pertaining to the senses. ***Ear nose and throat agents*** are used to treat a variety of disease states and symptoms. Selection of an agent is based on the condition being treated. Ophthalmic (eye) and otic (ear) formations include drops and ointments. Medications for these routes may have anti-infective properties such as Ciprofloxacin. Medication for the nose are used to treat allergy symptoms or nasal congestion these medications may be taking long-term, seasonally or for a few days.

Chart 1.7.e

Stems for Ear, Nose Eyes and Throat Agents

Stem	Description	Drug Example
-astine	H1 receptor	azelastine
-olol	Beta antagonists	betaxolol
-onide	Corticosteroid	budesonide

Endocrine Agents

The *endocrine system* is a collection of glands of an organism that secrete hormones directly into the circulatory system to be carried towards distant target organs. Endocrine agents treat a variety of diseases states within the endocrine system. Review the table below for the list of stems related to endocrine agents.

Stems for Endocrine Agents

Stem	Description	Drug Example
-formin	Hypoglycemic	Metformin
-glinide	Meglitinide	Repaglinide
-gliptin	Dipeptidyl peptidase	Saxagliptin
-glitazone	Thiazolidine	Rosiglitazone

Chart 1.7.f

Gastrointestinal Agents

Gastrointestinal agents include many different classes of drugs that are used to treat gastrointestinal disorders. Gastrointestinal agents can be used to treat conditions of the GI tract including constipation, diarrhea, GERD, heartburn, indigestion, nausea, spasms, ulcers and vomiting.

Gastrointestinal agents are reduced to three major categories. First, *anti-ulcer agents* act by reducing the stomach acid content either by directly neutralizing H+. Some anti-ulcer agents may act to coat existing ulcers to prevent further damage.

Second, *antiemetics* act on centers in the brain to reduce the incidence of vomiting. The final category serves to either speed up or slow down the intestinal system.

Chart 1.7.g

Stems for Gastrointestinal Agents

Stem	Description	Drug Example
-prazole	Antiulcer agent	lansoprazole
-setron	Serotonin 5-HT3	ondansetron
-tidine	H2 receptor antagonists	famotidine

Musculoskeletal and Osteoporosis

Skeletal muscle relaxants have been approved for either treatment of spasticity or for treatment of musculoskeletal conditions. Medications, physical therapy, and sometimes surgery can help reduce pain and maintain joint movement.

Pharmacologic agents used in the treatment of osteoarthritis include the following:

- Acetaminophen & Opioids
- Nonsteroidal anti-inflammatory drugs (NSAIDs)
- Intra-articular corticosteroids
- Intra-articular sodium hyaluronate
- Duloxetine
- Muscle relaxants

Stems for Musculoskeletal and Osteoporosis Medications

Stem	Description	Drug Example
-ac	Anti-inflammatory agents	diclofenac
-caine	Local anaesthetics	lidocaine
-coxib	Cox 2 inhibitor	celecoxib
-dronate	Bisphosphonates	Ibandronate
-icam	Anti-inflammatory agents	piroxicam

Chart 1.7.h

Reproductive Agents

Reproductive agents are commonly associated with hormone therapy. Women are prescribed agents that may contain a form of progestin and estrogen or a combination of both. Progestin are used to treat conditions such as abnormal vaginal bleeding or an overgrowth of the uterus lining. Estrogen on the other hand are typically prescribed to regulate hormonal imbalances. Estrogen can be used to treat symptoms of menopause and aid in the treatment of certain breast cancers. Testosterone is prescribed to men to treat symptoms of low testosterone. Typical side effects are reproductive agents include headaches, mood disorders, anxiety, fluid retention, weight gain and menstrual irregularities.

Stems for Reproductive Agents   Chart 1.7.i

Stem	Description	Drug Example
estr-	Estrogen	estradiol

Respiratory Agents

Respiratory agent is a term used to describe a wide variety of medicines used to relieve, treat, or prevent respiratory diseases such as asthma, chronic bronchitis, chronic obstructive pulmonary disease (COPD), or pneumonia.

Respiratory agents are available in many different forms, such as oral tablets, oral liquids, injections or inhalants. Inhalants deliver the required medicine or medicines directly to the lungs, which means the medicine(s) can act directly on the lung tissues, minimizing systemic side effects.

Some products contain more than one medicine (for example, inhalers that combine a long-acting bronchodilator with a glucocorticoid).

Stems for Respiratory Agents

Stem	Description	Drug Example
-ast	Antiasthmatics/ Antiallergics	montelukast
-astine	H1 receptors antagonists	azelastine
-tadine	H1 receptors antagonists	loratadine
-terol	Bronchodilators	albuterol

Chart 1.7.j

Genitourinary Tract Agents

The urinary system performs functions related to the removal of waste products and fluid balance maintenance including electrolyte and pH balances medications in this category can be prescribed to relieve urinary difficulty or treat painful urination. ***Genitourinary tract agents*** are medicines, which are used to treat conditions of the reproductive organs and excretory system or urinary tract. They include medicines used for bladder spasms, urinary pH modifiers, medicines for erectile dysfunction in men and medicines that suppress uterine contractions to prevent preterm labor.

Stems for Urinary System Agents

Chart 1.7.k

Stem	Description	Drug Example
-afil	PDE Inhibitors	Sildenafil
-steride	Testosterone reductase	dutasteride

Chapter 1: *Pharmacology for Pharmacy Technician*

Worksheet 1a: Pharmacology for PhT

1. Herbal and dietary supplements are regulated under the same statutes as OTC drugs by the U.S. Food and Drug Administration. True or false?

   True   **False**

2. List the three (3) characteristics of both terms below:

Brand Names	Generic Names

3. _____ is designated when two drug products meet strict criteria in accordance with the Food and Drug Administration (FDA) Orange Book.
   a) Pharmaceutical contraindications
   b) Therapeutic equivalence
   c) Pharmaceutical equivalents

4. Jason is a 15 year old with a history of non-allergic asthma and had been prescribed Xopenex HFA for 5 years. Currently, he was prescribed montelukast for allergies. According to the information in his patient medical history, what can you infer about this patient's prescriptions?

   _____

   _____

   _____

Chapter 1: *Pharmacology for Pharmacy Technician*

Worksheet 1b: Pharmacology for PhT

5. Complete the Venn diagram for the following terms:
   drug-nutrient interaction and drug-dietary supplement interaction

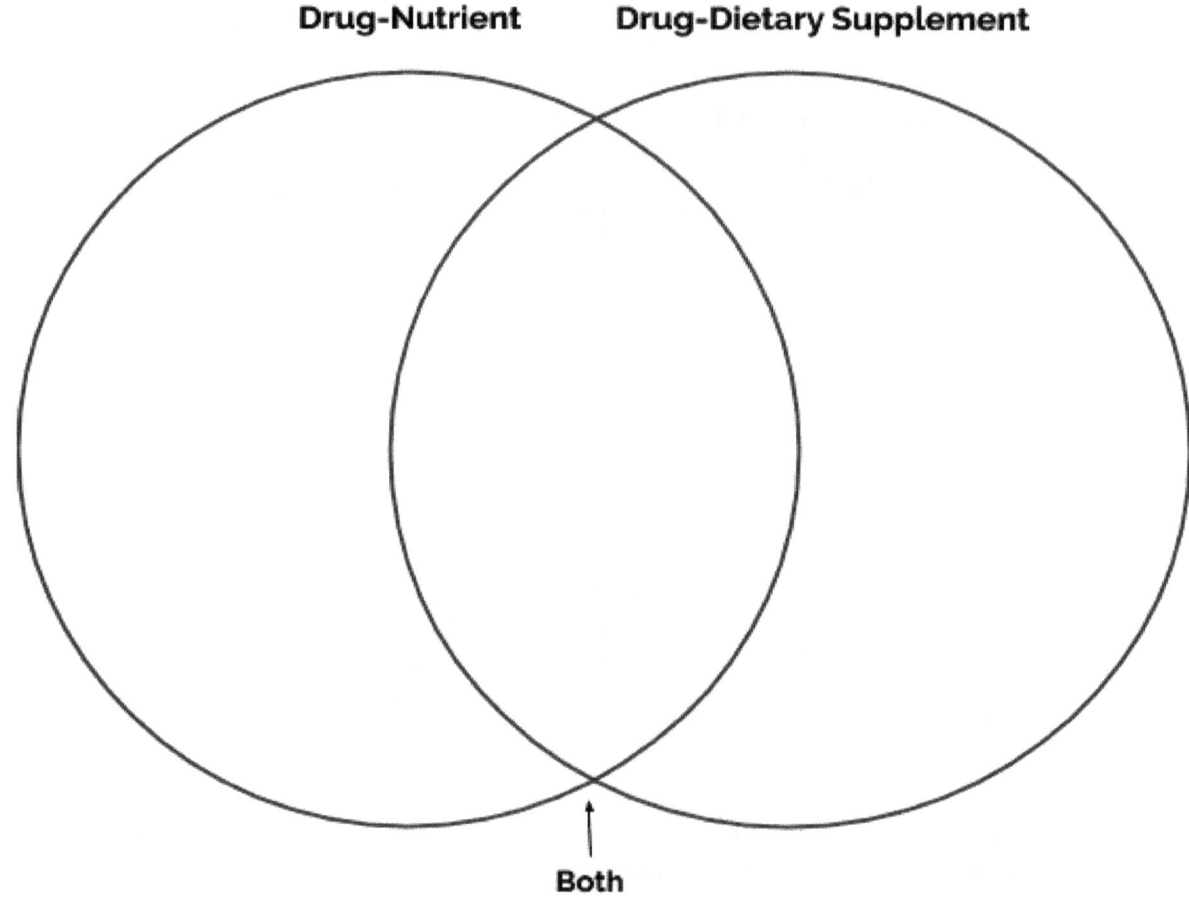

Drug-Nutrient   **Drug-Dietary Supplement**

↑
Both

6. Mr. Barnes was previously using both doxazosin and Proscar three months ago. Prior to lab tests requested by his oncologist, Mr. Barnes had taken the last of his remaining Proscar. If his results were to be interpreted without the knowledge of the patient resuming Proscar, the lab would need to be watchful for a _____ interaction.

7. Match the following colors of Coumadin to its strength:

Tan	Peach	Pink	Lavender	Blue	Teal	Lime Green	Yellow	White

| 2mg | 3mg | 5mg | 1mg | 7.5mg | 2.5mg | 4mg | 10mg | 6mg |

Chapter 1: *Pharmacology for Pharmacy Technician*

Worksheet 1c: Pharmacology for PhT

8. A gel is an example of a suspension dosage form. True or false?

   True   **False**

9. Patient X has been prescribed albuterol for asthma. Which of the following administration routes are common for albuterol?
   a) Tablet
   b) Inhalant
   c) A and B

10. Patients with acute problems, like pain or infection, may need a _____ duration of drug therapy.

11. List the three (3) facts of both terms below:

Common Side Effects	**Severe Side Effects**

12. Yasmin is a 7 year old who recently had chickenpox for the first time. Yasmin's mother is hesitant about giving her aspirin for a headache. It has been reported that young children whom were previously diagnosed with chickenpox or the flu have developed Reye's syndrome after consumption of aspirin. According to the report, <u>what</u> undesirable drug effect should her mother be concerned about? <u>Why</u> should her mother be concerned?

_____

_____

Worksheet 1d: Pharmacology for PhT

13. Match the following stems to their description:

<u>-afil</u>   <u>-arone</u>   <u>-ast</u>   <u>-caine</u>   <u>-conazole</u>   <u>-olol</u>   <u>-prazole</u>   <u>-terol</u>   <u>-vir</u>

Anti-arrhythmics   Anti-asthmatics/allergics   Anti-fungals   Anti-ulcer agents   Anti-viral

Beta blockers/antagonists   Bronchodilators   Local anesthesias   PDE Inhibitors

14. Fill in two (2) similarities and differences for the following terms: anti<u>viral</u> and anti<u>retro</u>viral

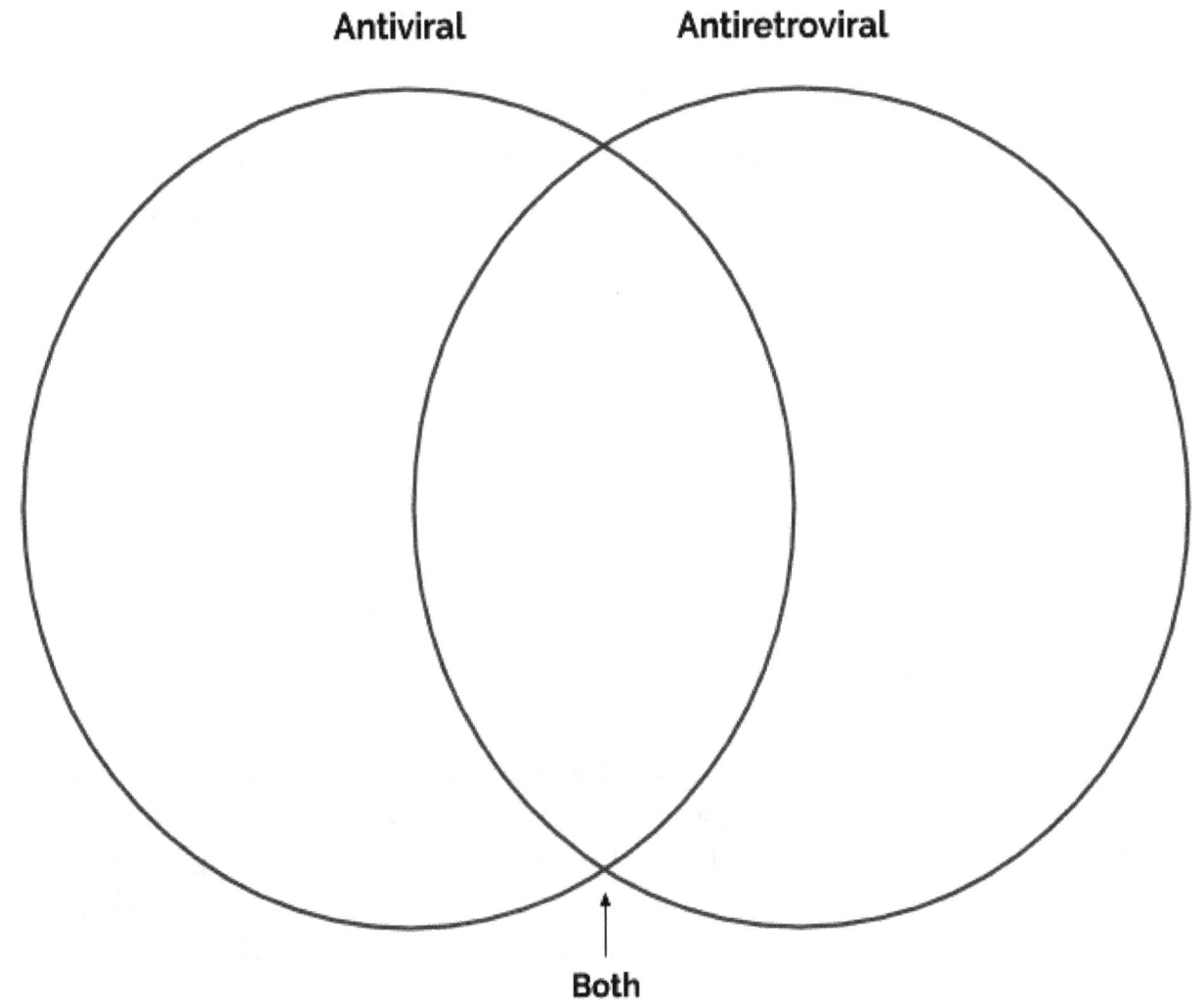

Both

Chapter 1: *Pharmacology for Pharmacy Technician*

Pharmacology for Pharmacy Technicians Quiz

1. Which of the following medications is a beta blocker used for the treatment of hypertension?
    a) Diltiazem
    b) Lisinopril
    c) Metoprolol

2. Azithromycin is classified as a bacteriostatic anti-infective agent. Which of the following drugs also has bacteriostatic properties?
    a) Cephalexin
    b) Erythromycin
    c) Levofloxacin

3. Medicines ending in the USAN approved suffix "-afil" are used to treat _____."
    a) Gout
    b) Hyperlipidemia
    c) Impotence

4. A suppository is a solid formulation used for what type of administration?
    a) Intravenous
    b) Oral
    c) Rectal

5. A branch of pharmacology referring to the biological and physical effects of the drug on the body is referred to as _____.
    a) Pharmacodynamics
    b) Pharmacokinetics
    c) Pharmacotherapeutics

6. Which of the following medications does NOT have a formulation that is available Over-the-counter?
    a) Acyclovir
    b) Fluticasone
    c) Loperamide

7. Which of the following drug interactions would be characterized as a relative contraindication?
    a) Diazepam and grapefruit juice
    b) Warfarin and aspirin
    c) Tetracycline and dairy products

8. *Helicobacter pylori* is a type of bacteria associated with the formation and/or exacerbation of the following disease states?
    a) Acne vulgaris
    b) Peptic ulcer disease
    c) Oral thrush

9. Which of the following medications is indicated in the treatment of epilepsy?
    a) Lansoprazole
    b) Levetiracetam
    c) Levofloxacin

10. According to Mrs. MacGuierre's patient medical history, she had been taking arginine within the last 6 months before being diagnosed with shingles. Mrs. McGuire is now prescribed acyclovir. What type of drug interaction would occur if combined?
    a) Drug-Drug Interaction
    b) Drug-Dietary Supplement Interaction
    c) Drug-Nutrient Interaction

Chapter 1: *Pharmacology for Pharmacy Technician*

Quiz: Study Guide

Question Number	Section Reference
1	1.1; 1.7
2	1.7
3	1.7
4	1.4; 1.5
5	1.7
6	1.7
7	1.3; 1.6 & 1.7
8	1.7
9	1.7
10	1.1; 1.2 & 1.3

Chapter References

Figure 1.1.a: https://www.ambien.com/ambien-cr; Figure 1.1.b: http://flaglerfreeclinic.org/PSDF/Pharmacy/P-Metoprolol-Tartrate.htm; Figure 1.1.c: https://www.fda.gov/files/image003.jpg; Figure 1.1.d: https://ntp.niehs.nih.gov/images/botanicals_graphic.png

Figure 1.2.a: https://bookstore.gpo.gov/sites/default/files/styles/product_page_image/public/covers/600_-_917-052-00000-0.jpg?itok=z0r8_QDh; Figure 1.2.b: composed illustration by author; Figure 1.2.c: https://printabletemplates.com/wp-content/uploads/templates/medical-history-form/medical%20history%20form%2001-768x994.jpg

Figure 1.3.a,b,c,e,g: https://aidsinfo.nih.gov/understanding-hiv-aids/glossary/765/drug-interaction&sa=D&ust=1561940574158000&usg=AFQjCNGWAEwxBSfW0yeJbZ3ATAzJLe5W5w;
Figure 1.3.d: https://www.walmart.com/nco/Bayer-Pain-Reliever-Aspirin-Bundle/47223815?wmlspartner%3Dwlpa%26selectedSellerId%3D0&sa=D&ust=15619406582820000&usg=AFQjCNHf4dvyUMvh8Z_35PwmhbWWMG5VFQ;
Figure 1.3.f: https://www.alamy.com/female-scientific-researcher-or-blood-test-assistant-at-work-in-laboratory-science-medicine-and-pharmacy-concept-image225660855.html&sa=D&ust=1561940847499000&usg=AFQjCNG7xA23UoyHEk1ROSBnhvz1vKeI-Q

Figure 1.4.a: https://i1.wp.com/www.aliem.com/wp-content/uploads/2016/12/Warfarin-pills-chart.jpg?resize=400%2C149&ssl=1;; Figure 1.4.b: http://www.coumadin.bmscustomerconnect.com/servlet/servlet.FileDownload?file=00Pi000000WLHVFEA5 (modified for reuse):

Table 1.4.a: composed illustration by author

Diagram 1.6.a: composed diagram by author

Chart 1.7.a-k: composed chart by author

Chapter 2

Pharmacy Law and Regulations

Rx Health Academy

General Information

A pharmacy practice involves many laws and regulations. Over 12% of the questions on the PTCB exam deal with them, so follow the outline below as you study. If there are areas in which you think you need additional practice or help, please reach out to your instructor.

Chapter 2: *Pharmacy Law and Regulations*

What you'll learn in this chapter

- Storage, handling, and disposal of hazardous substances and wastes
- Hazardous substances exposure, prevention and treatment
- Controlled substance transfer regulations and documentation requirements for receiving, ordering, returning, loss/theft, destruction
- Formula to verify the validity of a prescriber's DEA number
- Record keeping, documentation, and record retention
- Restricted drug programs and related prescription-processing requirements
- Professional standards related to data integrity, security, and confidentiality
- Requirement for consultation
- FDA's recall classification
- Infection control standards
- Record keeping for repackaged and recalled products and supplies
- Professional standards regarding the roles and responsibilities of pharmacists, pharmacy technicians, and other pharmacy employees
- Reconciliation between state and federal laws and regulations
- Facility, equipment, and supply requirements

Chapter Outline

2.1 Routine Practices With Hazardous Substances And Waste
2.2 Controlled Substance Documentation
2.3 Professional Standards
2.4 FDA Recall Classification
2.5 Pharmacy Personnel Roles
2.6 Facility Requirements
2.7 Reference Materials

2.1 ROUTINE PRACTICES WITH HAZARDOUS SUBSTANCES AND WASTE

Hazardous materials can be defined as any chemical or drug that poses potential harm to the person preparing or coming in contact with it. The Occupational Safety and Health Administration (OSHA) has standards to protect employees who work with hazardous materials. This includes proper *personal protective equipment* (PPE) and procedures for dealing with different types of hazardous substances. Often, manufacturers of such products send written documentation, known as *Material Safety Data Sheets* (MSDS), that outline appropriate handling, storage requirements, and cleanup procedures for the hazardous product.

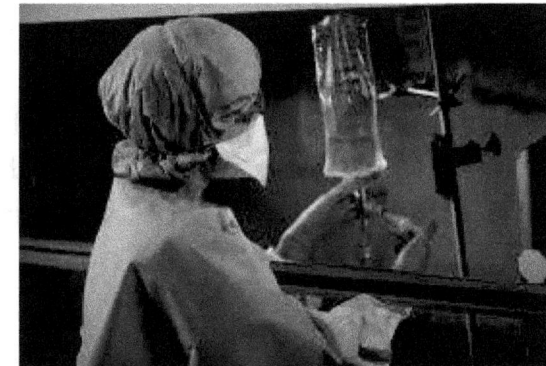

Figure 2.1.a

Storage

The storage requirements of hazardous materials are often dependent on the type of material. Regardless of the type, hazardous materials and chemicals should be stored separately from other materials. Often, they can be stored in a negative pressure room where they will later be handled.

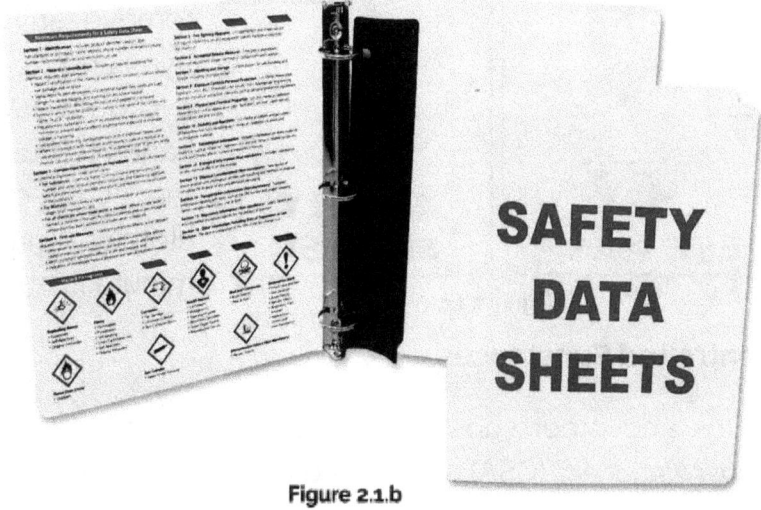

Figure 2.1.b

Handling

Extreme caution should be used when handling a hazardous material. When near, or in contact with, any of these types of materials, you need to use personal protective wear as outlined in the MSDS for that specific product.

Disposal

Disposal of hazardous waste must be separate from the disposal of other waste and the waste must be labeled as "hazardous drug waste." It also needs to be stored in a leakproof container that is labeled as such until it is disposed of safely.

Exposure to Hazardous Substances

In case of accidental exposure to hazardous material, you should be aware of the equipment available in your workplace to emergently help minimize exposure and injury. This could include an eyewash station, shower, or other emergent cleaning mechanism. Follow the instructions on the MSDS for the specific product with which you are working. Follow all instructions for cleanup of hazardous materials, including the use of specific spill kits that allow you to safely clean the product. It is also important to report any incidents to your supervisor.

Exposure Prevention

Always use caution when manipulating or using any hazardous materials. Follow the instructions on the MSDS for the product and the safety regulations of your specific work area. If unsure of the appropriate procedure for storing or handling materials, ask your supervisor. Doing so can help prevent accidental exposure

Treatment for Exposure

Depending on the type of chemical and level of exposure, the management may vary. Always inform your supervisor of an accidental exposure and follow the recommendations outlined in the MSDS for the product you are using. In the event of facial or eye contact with a hazardous substance, remove any contact lenses prior to washing out the eyes and do not reinsert the lenses. Use the appropriate eye wash station to irrigate your eyes. If unavailable, use hands to flush eyes with water for at least 15 minutes. In the event of skin contact, remove any contaminated clothing immediately and rinse the area for at least 15 minutes.

Figure 2.1.c

Controlled Substances

Drugs and other substances that are considered controlled substances under the *Controlled Substances Act* (CSA) are divided into five schedules.

Substances (drugs) are placed in their respective schedules based on whether they have a currently accepted medical use in treatment in the United States, their relative abuse potential, and likelihood of causing dependence when abused.

The *Controlled Substances Act of 1970*, regulates the distribution and use of addictive drugs, or those having a high potential for abuse. Drug abuse and addiction will be discussed later in the course. The *Drug Enforcement Administration (DEA)* enforces this act. It divides addictive drugs into five categories, of schedules,based on their potential physical and psychological dependence.

Chapter 2: *Pharmacy Law and Regulations*

Schedule	Description	Example
Schedule 1	Drugs in this schedule have no accepted medical use in the United States	Heroin
Schedule II	Drugs in this schedule have an extremely high abuse potential with severe likelihood of physical and psychological dependence. They do have accepted medical uses.	Morphine, cocaine, meperidine (Demerol)
Schedule III	Drugs in this schedule have a lower abuse potential than the drugs in Schedule II.	Codeine in combination with aspirin or acetaminophen
Schedule IV	Drugs in this schedule have a low abuse potential compared to the drugs in Schedule II.	Diazepam (Valium)
Schedule V	Drugs in this schedule have the lowest abuse potential and consist primarily of codeine cough preparations	Elixir of terpin hydrate with codeine

Chart 2.1.a

Controlled substance prescriptions have specific requirements.

All prescriptions for controlled substances must include the following:

- Date the prescription was issued
- Prescriber's signature
- Patient's full name and address
- Medication name
- Strength
- Dosage form
- Quantity prescribed
- Directions for use
- Prescriber's name, address, and registration number.

Schedule III and IV controlled substances expire after 6 months.

Schedule III and IV controlled substances cannot be filled or refilled more than 5 times or more than 6 months after the date the prescription was issued, whichever occurs first. Schedule II prescriptions cannot be <u>refilled</u>. Under federal law, there is no expiration for a Schedule II prescription. However, many states have established time restrictions. In states with no expiration this becomes a tricky situation and the pharmacist's professional judgement is extremely important.

Schedule II controlled substances can be dispensed through an oral prescription for emergencies.

The following requirements must be followed when dispensing Schedule II controlled substances for emergency situations:

- The quantity prescribed and dispensed must be limited to an adequate amount to treat the patient during the emergency.
- The pharmacist must document the oral prescription information and verify the identity of the prescribing practitioner.
- The pharmacy must receive the written prescription within 7 days, and it must state on the face "Authorization for Emergency Dispensing" with the date of the oral order.
- The pharmacist must attach the paper prescription to the emergency oral authorization. Pharmacists must document electronic prescriptions with the original authorization and date of the oral order.
- Pharmacists must notify the Drug Enforcement Administration if a prescriber fails to deliver the written or electronic prescription on time.

Controlled Substances Transfer

Schedule II

Schedule II drugs cannot be transferred.

Schedule III-V

Schedule III-V drugs can be transferred between pharmacies <u>one time</u>, unless the pharmacies share an online, real-time database. In that case, the prescription can be transferred between the two locations until it expires or there are no refills left. All transfers must occur between two pharmacists. The prescription should be voided by the original pharmacy after transfer and a notation that it is a transferred prescription should be written by the current pharmacy. The following need to be included when transferring a prescription:

- original prescription date and dispensing date
- number of refills remaining
- the name of the transferring pharmacist
- the DEA number, name, and address of the transferring pharmacy

2.2 CONTROLLED SUBSTANCE DOCUMENTATION

According to the *Comprehensive Drug Abuse Prevention and Control Act of 1970* (also commonly referred to the *Controlled Substances Act of 1970*), all controlled substances need to maintain accurate and up to date records and inventory. A complete and accurate inventory of all controlled substances helps maintain the pharmacy's inventory and keeps the pharmacy aligned with federal regulations. It can also help prevent drug diversion and misuse of medications. The regulations for record-keeping can be broken up into three categories: *schedule II, schedule III-V, and non-controlled substances.* The following documentation guidelines focus only on the requirements of the first two groups.

Ordering

The *Drug Enforcement Administration (DEA)* is a United States federal law enforcement agency under the United States Department of Justice, tasked with combating drug trafficking and distribution within the United States. As apart of this enforcement the DEA monitors the distribution of controlled substances using a series of forms.

Schedule II

Schedule II must be ordered using a *DEA 222 form*. This form is specific to Schedule II drugs, must be completed in triplicate, and can be handwritten or typed. The three copies are retained by different stops in the supply chain to ensure consistency. The top copy is for the supplier of the schedule II medications, the middle copy is sent to the DEA, and the bottom copy is sent back to the purchaser. Once filled out, the DEA 222 form is valid only for 60 days. A maximum of 10 different medications can be ordered on one form, and the form must be signed by the pharmacist who is registered with the DEA. The registrant pharmacist is typically the pharmacist in charge or the pharmacy manager.

Alternatively, a *Controlled Substance Ordering System* (CSOS) can be used in place of a DEA 222 form for ordering Schedule II drugs. The pharmacy must meet specific electronic requirements to ensure digital security when using the CSOS.

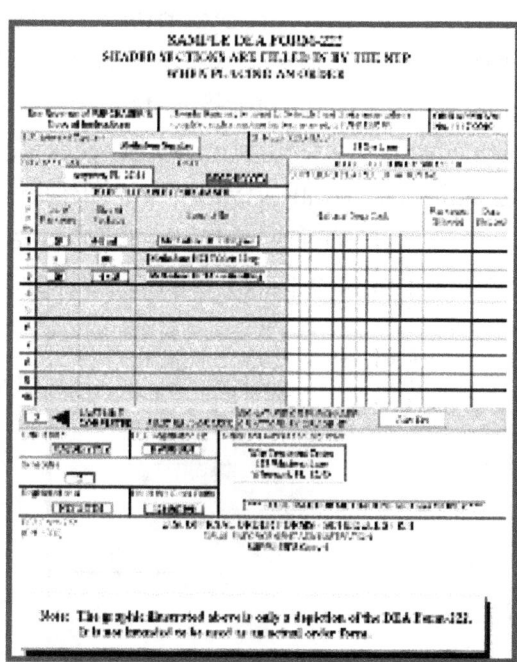

Figure 2.2.a

Schedule III-V

There are no special ordering requirements for Schedule III-V drugs. They can be ordered through the same mechanism as non-controlled medications.

Receiving

Schedule II

After receiving an order, the pharmacist in charge must verify each item and document the date each was received on copy three of the original order form that accompanies the order. Copy 3 of each order form must be maintained in the pharmacy for at least 2 years.

Schedule III-V

There are no special receiving requirements for Schedule III-V drugs. Follow the rules for non-controlled drugs.

Returning

Controlled substances may be returned to the supplier. The pharmacy must fill out a DEA 222 form to return Schedule II drugs.

Loss/Theft

In the event of lost or stolen controlled substances II-V, the DEA and local law enforcement must be notified immediately. The pharmacist must then fill out a **DEA 106 form** that details the medications involved in the theft. The original form is sent to the DEA and a copy should be retained for the pharmacy's records. Spilling a small amount of a liquid or breaking a few tablets does not need to be reported. Only a *significant* loss of controlled substances requires a DEA 106 form.

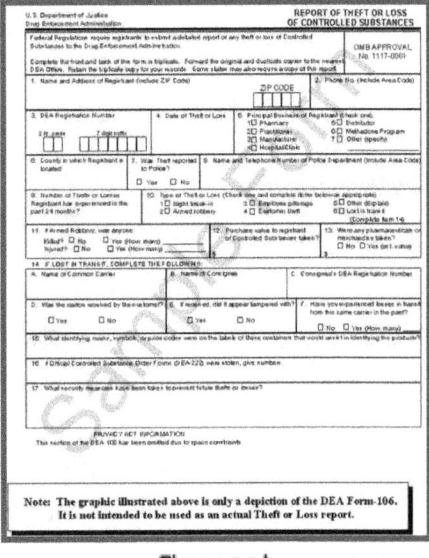

Figure 2.2.b

Destruction

Outdated, damaged, or unwanted controlled substances may be destroyed under the authorization of the DEA. To destroy the medications, the pharmacy or distributor must fill out a **DEA 41 form**. The form must contain:

- dates, location, and method of destruction
- **National Drug Code** (NDC), name, strength, dosage form, and quantity of the medications being destroyed
- signatures of two witnesses of the destruction (should be employees)

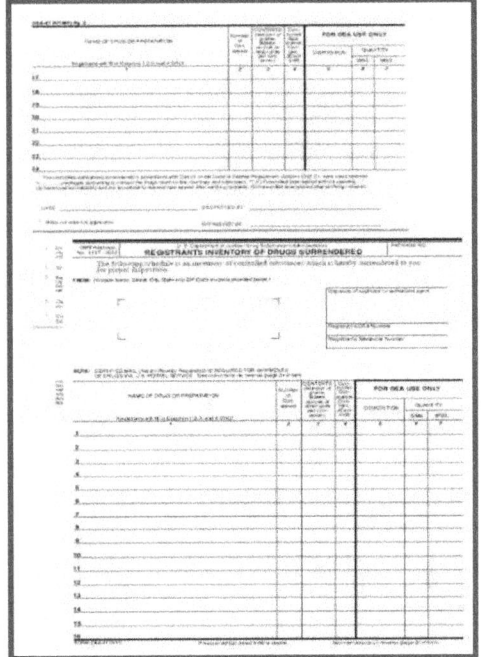

Figure 2.2.c

National Drug Code (NDC) Example 2.2.a

Every NDC number has 3 segments.

0339 - 4164 - 06

The **First segment** of an NDC number string identifies the drug's **Manufacturer**. This number is unique to the maker or re-packager of the product.

0339 - **4164** - 06

The **Second segment** of an NDC number string identifies the **Product**. This number is unique to the formulation and strength of the product.

0339 - 4164 - **06**

The **Third segment** of an NDC number string identifies the **Packaging**. This number is unique to the size and quantity of the product.

DEA Number Validation

To prescribe controlled substances, a provider must have a valid DEA number. It is the responsibility of the pharmacist to verify the DEA number as being accurate. In general, the DEA number consists of two letters followed by seven numbers. The first letter identifies the type of DEA registrant and the second number is the first letter of the prescriber's last name.

To verify the DEA number, follow these steps:

Step	Description
1	Add the first, third, and fifth numbers together.
2	Add the second, fourth, and sixth numbers together.
3	Multiply the sum in the second step by 2.
4	Add the total from steps 1 and 3 together.
5	Verify that the second digit of the sum in step 4 is the same as the last digit of the prescriber's DEA number.

Chart 2.2.a

DEA Verification Example 2.2.b

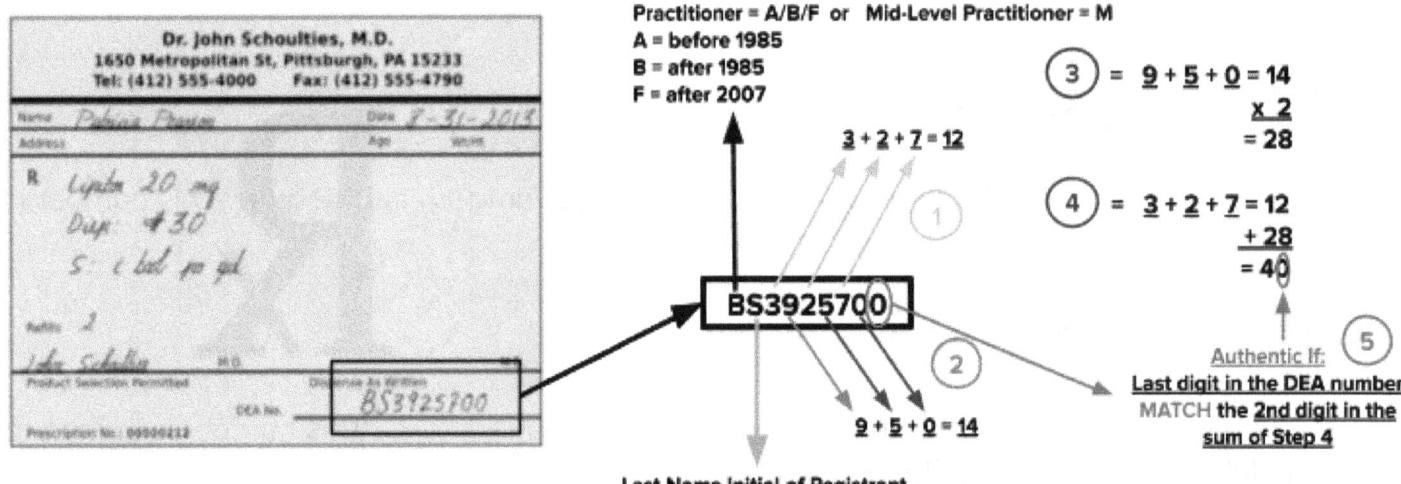

Prescription Record

Proper record keeping is one of the most important aspects of pharmacy practice. It helps to ensure the accuracy of prescription processing, inventory, and all the important aspects of pharmacy operations. Pharmacies are required to maintain and keep organized records for all prescriptions, including controlled substances.

Record Keeping and Documentation

All records should be kept in an organized and accurate fashion. Prescriptions records must have the patient's name and address, drug name, strength, quantity, and date dispensed. Any controlled substance prescriptions should be marked as such and should be stored in accordance with state law. If unspecified by state law, there should be three separate files: *C II*, *C III-V*, and *non-controlled*

Record Retention

Pharmacies must keep records of all prescriptions for a <u>minimum of 5 years</u>. They must be organized in such a way that they can easily be inspected by the DEA or state BOP.

Figure 2.2.d

Restricted Drugs

Some medications can be harmful if taken by the wrong patients, such as people who are pregnant or have a specific disease that would be a contraindication for use of that drug. As such, certain potentially harmful medications have specific criteria that must be met before the prescription can be filled. The *Risk Evaluation and Mitigation Strategies* (REMS)

Program between the FDA and drug manufacturers helps limit inappropriate dispensing and protects patients.

Each drug has different criteria that must be met and this can include patient education, elements for safe use of the medication, a communication plan between healthcare providers and the patient, laboratory tests, etc.

One example is isotretinoin, which can be very teratogenic if given to a pregnant woman. The Isotretinoin Safety and Risk Management Act outlines the requirements to prevent disastrous effects. The law requires patients to have a blood test and be counseled on safe use before being given a prescription. The patient also has a 7-day time frame in which to fill his or her prescription and can only be given a 30-day supply.

2.3 PROFESSIONAL STANDARDS

All personnel involved in pharmacy practice are required to uphold a level of professionalism consistent with the standards of practice. This includes a professional demeanor, respect for patients, and communication with other healthcare providers and the general public. These standards also extend to using discretion with sensitive medical information. All patient personal information needs to be protected and maintained properly.

Data Integrity

The integrity of all pharmacy records must be maintained accurately and in an organized manner so that specific records can easily be accessed. Maintaining the integrity of the data includes electronic records of all prescriptions, orders, invoices, controlled substances, etc. All records must also be retained in hard copy form to ensure proper archiving of data.

Security

The security of medications and medication records is vital to protect sensitive patient information. All pharmacies need to have a monitored security system that signifies any type of intrusion in real time. It may also be wise to use video surveillance within the pharmacy to prevent drug diversion. All pharmacies should also be equipped with physical barriers that prevent entry into the pharmacy during non-operational hours. This may include barred doors and windows or a lockable steel gate.

Confidentiality

All members of the pharmacy staff must keep all patient information confidential. They should only discuss information required to care for the patient and this should only occur in the pharmacy and out of hearing distance from any other patients. The *Health Insurance Portability and Accountability Act* (HIPAA) set the standards for disclosing sensitive patient information. The act states that any information that can be used to identify a patient must be protected. All pharmacy personnel must be trained on HIPAA laws and take steps to limit any use of personal patient information. If this information is released or used outside of the normal prescription process, that patient whose information was disclosed must be notified.

Figure 2.3.a

Consultation Requirements

As part of their practice, pharmacists are required to provide counseling to patients on their medications. The *Omnibus Budget Reconciliation Act of 1990* (OBRA 90) defines the expectations for pharmacist consultation. OBRA 90 also dictates proper pharmacy record-keeping and requires drug utilization review of all prescriptions. It is important to note that while only a pharmacist can provide counseling, any member of the pharmacy staff can make the offer to counsel. This means that pharmacy technicians can ask the patient if they would like counseling but cannot perform the counseling. Topics pharmacists must cover during counseling include: drug name/description, how to take the medication and what it is for, common side effects or interactions with drugs or food, proper medication storage, refill information, and what to do in the event of a missed dose.

2.4 FDA RECALL CLASSIFICATION

Figure 2.4.a

The *Food and Drug Administration* (FDA) may request a drug manufacturer to recall or remove a drug from the market for commercial use. There are a variety or reasons a drug can be recalled including problems with the dosage form or adverse reactions related to the specific medication.

There are three types of FDA recalls: (Note: If there is a recall the FDA will notify patients)

Chart 2.4.a

Class	Description
Class I	is the most severe type of recall and involves medication that is likely to cause severe adverse effects or even death. This can also occur if one drug is labeled as another drug.
Class II	occurs when medication may cause temporary adverse health effects that are reversible or if there is a small risk of serious adverse effects.
Class III	is the least severe type of recall. The medication in question is not likely to cause a patient to have adverse effects.

Chapter 2: *Pharmacy Law and Regulations*

Infection Control

Infection control procedures are incredibly important because they can prevent the spread of bacterial, fungal, and viral infections in a variety of healthcare settings. Pharmacy technicians can play a large role in preventing the spread of infections to patients by using appropriate techniques and following regulations. The *Occupational Safety and Health Administration* (OSHA) sets the standards for the safety and protection of all personnel working in the pharmacy.

Figure 2.4.b

Any contact with prescription products must have a mechanism for personal protection as outlined in OSHA. Other guidelines of United States Pharmacopeia (USP) chapter 797 and chapter 795 outline the requirements for sterile and non-sterile compounding including work environment, maintaining sterility, and personal protective gear.

The United States Pharmacopeia (USP) is a pharmacopeia for the United States published annually by the United States Pharmacopeial Convention.

- The *"USP DI Volume I"* contains drug Information for healthcare professionals.
- The *"USP DI Volume II"* contains advice for patients and drug information.
- The *"USP-NF"* is a combination of two compendia, the United States Pharmacopeia (USP) and the National Formulary (NF).

Figure 2.4.c

Regulations

Three main sets of regulations set the standard for infection control related to pharmacy practice including OSHA, USP chapter 795, and USP chapter 797. Generally, these guidelines describe the techniques for drug manipulation, environmental standards, and personal protection related to <u>sterile and non-sterile compounding</u>.

- OSHA outlines how to protect the person doing the drug manipulation such as a pharmacist or pharmacy technician. This includes personal protective equipment such as gloves, gowns, hair and beard covers, and eye protection.
- USP 795 describes the techniques, equipment, and work area requirements for non-sterile compounding.
- USP 797 describes the techniques, equipment, and work area requirements for sterile compounding. Appropriate personal cleaning and protective wear requirements are also a large part of the 797 guidelines.

Environmental Standards

Prior to any contact with prescription medications, pharmacy technicians must make sure the work area meets the standards appropriate as outlined in OSHA, USP 795, or USP 797. This includes verifying that the practice environment is clean. This could be as simple as cleaning counting trays or as complex as a full clean room for sterile compounding. Specifics for each type of compounding are listed below:

Non-sterile Compounding

- *Hand-washing:* It should occur before putting on any gloves or personal protective equipment. It is the first step anytime you come into contact with prescription materials.
- *Clean equipment and counter:* Having a clean workspace will prevent contamination of the medications you are dispensing. All equipment and work spaces should be cleaned before any work is done.

Sterile Compounding

- *Clean room:* The *clean room* is a sterilized workspace specifically used for manipulation of medications and compounding. Pharmacy Technicians working in the clean room are required to wear appropriate protective equipment as described in USP 797. Due to the sterile nature of the clean room, pharmacy workers should try to avoid coming and going as much as possible to prevent unwanted dust or bacteria from entering the clean room.
- *Laminar flow hood:* The flow hood is the sterile area of the clean room where drug compounding, such as making IV's, occurs. Air is blown horizontally across the workspace to prevent bacteria or other materials from tarnishing the drug product. The *High-efficiency Particulate Air filter* (HEPA) is a key component of the laminar flow hood. Any particles are caught in the filter so they do not come in contact with the drug product

Product and Recall Records

In the event of a drug or product recall, a pharmacy must comply with the recall and keep accurate records to aid in the safety to patients that might have been affected. The state BOP and Joint Commission's recommendations must be followed. The pharmacist needs to contact all patients who might have been affected and reconcile the need for the recall. All recall records should be maintained in a similar manner as that for prescriptions.

2.5 PHARMACY PERSONNEL ROLES

Regardless of the setting, the roles of each member of the pharmacy staff should be clearly defined. These roles are delineated from state and federal laws as well as the Joint Commission recommendations for healthcare workers. The Board of Pharmacy defines what each member of the team is able to do from a practical and legal perspective.

Pharmacist

Pharmacists are responsible for the safety and accuracy of everything that happens within the pharmacy. As such, they are the person in charge and can further delegate responsibility to other pharmacy personnel. Pharmacy interns may have similar responsibilities as a pharmacist, but must be directly overseen by the pharmacist. Duties specific to the pharmacist include final prescription verification, prescription transfer, ordering of medications, and keeping accurate documentation. A pharmacist also performs the *Drug Utilization Review* (DUR) process which evaluates: therapeutic duplication, drug-disease contraindications, drug-drug interactions, incorrect drug dosage, incorrect duration of treatment, drug-allergy interactions, and clinical abuse/misuse of medication.

Figure 2.5.a

Pharmacy Technician

Figure 2.5.b

Pharmacy technicians can be involved in many aspects of pharmacy operations. Things technicians are *not* allowed to do include: Drug Utilization Review, patient counseling, transferring prescriptions, ordering and record keeping (all need pharmacist signature), and prescription verification (some states do allow tech-check-tech on a limited basis, however). All other aspects of pharmacy practice can involve technicians, including processing and filling prescriptions, compounding, maintaining inventory, and medication delivery.

Other Pharmacy Employees

Other people with access to the pharmacy and those working within the pharmacy should have defined roles. Without proper licensing as a technician, other personnel should not be involved in the medication distribution process except for performing cashier duties at the time of prescription sales. All confidentiality laws apply to *all* personnel working around sensitive patient information.

State vs. Federal Regulations

Although federal law covers all 50 states, each state may also have a specific set of laws to govern the practice of pharmacy. In some cases, the federal and state laws are not the same and may even conflict. In the event of a conflict, the more stringent law (whether it's state or federal) prevails and should be followed.

2.6 FACILITY REQUIREMENTS

All types of pharmacies have requirements for space and equipment which vary by the type of facility it is. The rules are governed by state boards of pharmacy and should be considered by all pharmacy personnel. A few standard requirements are also in place and are discussed below.

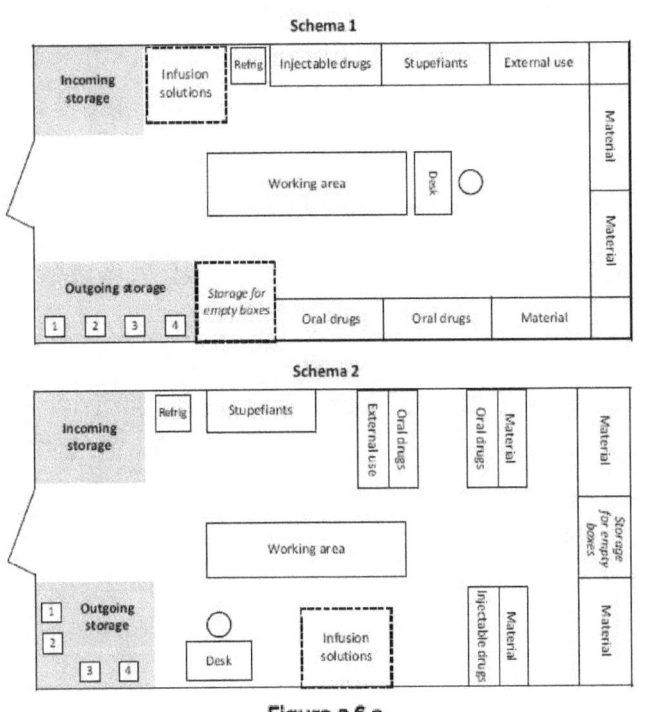

Figure 2.6.a

Space

All pharmacies are required to keep a clean, uncluttered, working space. State Boards of Pharmacies have specific requirements about the size of the pharmacy as well as required amounts of counter space and storage space. Federal law leaves these requirements up to each state individually. Check with your State Board of Pharmacy for more specific information.

Equipment

All pharmacies must have access to a cold and hot water supply within the pharmacy. There also needs to be a refrigerator for medication that requires temperature controlled storage. This must be separate from where all other types of perishables, such as lunches and beverages, are located. A safe or lockable device/area is required as well. Often this is used to store Schedule II controlled substances; however, C II medications do not have to be stored this way in all states. The pharmacy must also be equipped with a backup power supply in the event of a power failure.

Supply

Pharmacies should have the appropriate supplies for the type of setting. For example, a retail pharmacy needs to have vials, counting trays, spatulas, etc. There should also be an appropriate supply of medications to support the patients that use the pharmacy. Although it may not be feasible to have every possible drug option on hand, pharmacy staff should do their best to anticipate the medication needs of their patients.

Figure 2.6.a

Prescription File Storage

All prescriptions must be kept on-file at the pharmacy for a minimum of 5 years after the prescription was filled. There should be an electronic record as well as the hard copy of the prescriptions that are easily accessible. As such, prescriptions should be organized and separated, based on if they are written for controlled substances or non-controlled substances.

There are three options for how to file prescriptions:

Three separate files:
- Non-controlled
- C III-V
- C II

Two separate files:
- Non-controlled + C III-V
- C II

Two separate files:
- Non-controlled
- All Controlled (C II-V)

Cleanliness

Even though the hours of pharmacy operation may vary by setting, the pharmacy's cleanliness must be maintained in all types of work environments. The following things should be done at least daily, if not more often:

- dusting of equipment and medication storage areas
- wiping down of keyboards, phones, all working surfaces, and tools used for medication preparation and dispensing
- vacuuming or mopping the floors
- removing trash from the pharmacy work area
- cleaning patient areas (only some settings have direct patient care areas in or around the pharmacy)

2.7 REFERENCE MATERIALS

By law, all pharmacies are required to have specific reference materials on hand in order to legally operate. These can be available in print or electronic form and include all references that may be necessary for the pharmacist to adequately meet the needs of the patients served:

- a list of all laws, rules, and regulations that impact the pharmacy's practice
- a reference on drug interactions.
- the Orange Book
- a reference on natural or herbal medicines.

Additional Pharmacy Laws

The following laws are also important for the practice of pharmacy to help ensure patient safety and prevent drug diversion.

Figure 2.7.a

Pure Food and Drug Act of 1906

This act states that drugs must be pure and unadulterated and have to be labeled accurately. It also extends to food and drinks being marketed. It is important to note that this law does not address medication safety such as adverse effects, only that the medication is pure. Under this law a rug does not need to list ingredients, directions, or safety warnings.

Federal Food, Drug and Cosmetic Act of 1938 (FFDCA)

This law was enacted to improve upon the Pure Food and Drug Act after over one hundred deaths for an unsafe ingredient within an elixir on the market. The act requires all products to include a list ingredients, directions, and safety warnings. It also states that all drugs must be approved by the FDA prior to being marketed and used by patients. It outlines the labeling requirements for all prescription and over-the-counter medications. The law better defined misbranded and adulterated drugs as listed below:

- A product is considered misbranded if it is misrepresented on the label, contains unapproved color additives or ingredients, or does not comply with labeling and warning requirements as established by the FDA.
- A product is considered to be adulterated if it fails to comply with the standards for quality, strength, or purity.

Poison Prevention Packaging Act of 1970 (PPPA)

Figure 2.7.c

This act defines the level of product security needed to prevent children from accessing medication containers. It resulted from accidental poisonings of children who accidentally ingested medications. The requirement for child-resistant containers is that if given to a child, only 20% of children could access the medication inside. It is important to note that not every single product has to meet these requirements, however. For example, if a product is clearly labeled "not child resistant" then it is an exception. Certain medications can also be exceptions in limited doses.

Combat Methamphetamine Epidemic Act of 2005 (CMEA)

The CMEA places restrictions on the sale, storage, and record requirements for products containing ephedrine, pseudoephedrine, and phenylpropanolamine. The maximum amount that can be bought by an individual customer is 3.6 grams per day and 9 grams in a 30-day period.

Note that this refers to the base chemical, not the overall tablet strength of the product. The act also requires that any products containing ephedrine, pseudoephedrine, or phenylpropanolamine be kept behind the pharmacy counter to make sure all the required documentation is completed with the sale and to prevent theft. An electronic or written logbook must be kept detailing the personal information of the person purchasing the product and quantity, strength, date, and time of the product sale.

CMEA regulations & sale & purchase limitations for sellers

limitations on daily & monthly purchases | require photo ID for any purchase | personal record of all purchases for 2 years | limit customer access | detailed log of all product sales

Figure 2.7.d

Chapter 2: *Pharmacy Law and Regulations*

Worksheet 2a: Pharmacy Law and Regulation

1. Give an example for Schedule I-V Drugs that were not mentioned in **Chart 2.1.a**.

Schedule	Example

2. In the event of facial or eye contact with a hazardous substance, remove any _____ prior to washing out the eyes and do not reinsert the _____.

3. Label each schedule drug class from least abused to most abused.

    1 - Least   **2 - Less Likely**   **3 - Likely**   **4 - More Likely**   **5 - Most**

    _____   _____   _____   _____   _____

4. Label the manufacturer, product, and packaging segments of the following NDC number.

    NDC 4903 - 851 - 30

    _____ _____ _____

Chapter 2: *Pharmacy Law and Regulations*

Worksheet 2b: Pharmacy Law and Regulations

5. Verify the DEA number below:

   (Show your work)

   # B J 6 1 2 5 3 4 1

6. What does HIPPA stand for?

   a) Health Information Privacy Administration Act of 1990
   b) Health Insurance Privacy Administration Act of 1996
   c) Health Insurance Portability and Accountability Act of 1996

7. According to OBRA 90, a pharmacy technician is required to perform a consultation with a patient. True or false?

   True   **False**

8. Match the FDA recall class with its description.

Class III	**Class II**	**Class I**
Occurs when medication may cause temporary adverse health effects that are reversible or if there is a small risk of serious adverse effects.	The least severe type of recall. The medication in question is not likely to cause a patient to have adverse effects.	The most severe class and involves medication that is likely to cause severe adverse effects or death. This can also occur if one drug is labeled as another drug.

Pharmacy Law and Regulations Quiz

1. Which copy of the triplicate DEA 222 form does the purchaser retain?
   a) Copy 1 (top copy)
   b) Copy 2 (middle copy)
   c) Copy 3 (bottom copy)
   d) All copies are forwarded to the DEA

2. Which of the following statements is true regarding prescription refills?
   a) Schedule II prescriptions can be refilled up to 5 times in 6 months
   b) Schedule III prescriptions can be refilled up to 5 times in 6 months
   c) Schedule II prescriptions can be refilled up to 1 year
   d) Schedule III prescriptions can be refilled up to 1 year

3. According to federal law, how long must schedule III,IV, and V invoices be maintained in the pharmacy?
   a) 1 year
   b) 2 years
   c) 3 years
   d) 4 years

4. Which of the following is an example of a misbranded drug?
   a) The OTC product label is missing potential drug warnings
   b) The drug was manufactured in an unsanitary facility
   c) The drug leaves the pharmacy and is then re-dispensed
   d) The bottle contents are outdated

5. Oxycodone is an example of a drug in what controlled schedule?
   a) Schedule I
   b) Schedule II
   c) Schedule III
   d) Schedule IV

6. Which regulation was promoted, in part, due to the death of over a hundred individuals because of the addition of diethylene glycol to a sulfa-based elixir?
   a) Federal Food Drug and Cosmetic Act 1938
   b) Health Insurance Portability and Accountability Act of 1996
   c) Comprehensive Drug Abuse Prevention and Control Act of 1970
   d) Poison Prevention Packaging Act of 1970

Chapter 2: *Pharmacy Law and Regulations*

7. Which DEA form should be filled out in the event of a theft of a Schedule II substance
    a) DEA 222
    b) DEA 41
    c) DEA 106
    d) No form is needed

8. What are the maximum daily and monthly limits placed on the purchase of pseudoephedrine - containing products?
    a) 1.2g/day of base drug; 5g/month of base drug
    b) 2g/ day of based drug; 6g/month of base drug
    c) 2.8g/day of base drug; 7.5 g/month of base drug
    d) 3.6g/day of base drug; 9g/ month of base drug

9. What does REMS stand for ?
    a) Risk Evaluation and Mitigation Strategies
    b) Risk Effort and Medical Strategies
    c) Recovery Evaluation and Master Strategies

10. Which of the following reference books provides information directed toward the patient?
    a) USP- DI Volume 1
    b) USP- DI Volume 2
    c) USP-NF

Chapter 2: *Pharmacy Law and Regulations*

Quiz: Study Guide

Question Number	Section Reference
1	2.2
2	2.1
3	2.2
4	2.7
5	2.1
6	2.7
7	2.2
8	2.7
9	2.2
10	2.4

Chapter References

Figure 2.1.a: https://encrypted-tbn0.gstatic.com/images?q=tbn:ANd9GcTd0N42GJ5HQPNC4lvyMjERA2yw8jLW5KxR21ETRDXg7ktYOLgMbw;
Figure 2.1.b: https://www.osha-safety-training.net/wp-content/uploads/2013/11/new-SDS-binder-inside.jpg;
Figure 2.1.c: https://encrypted-tbn0.gstatic.com/images?q=tbn:ANd9GcT_0rKXaY3TLrTdM-hdEKnRvitgPfD1JPYf8kS95fO4FZsvcgEFcQ:
Chart 2.1.a: composed by author

Figure 2.2.a: https://www.deadiversion.usdoj.gov/pubs/manuals/narcotic/images/dea222c.gif;
Figure 2.2.b: https://www.deadiversion.usdoj.gov/pubs/manuals/narcotic/images/dea106p1.gif:
Figure 2.2.c: modified by author using images from https://www.deadiversion.usdoj.gov/pubs/manuals/pract/appendices/app_h/images/app_h_41.gif and
https://www.deadiversion.usdoj.gov/pubs/manuals/pract/appendices/app_h/images/app_h_41a.gif; Example 2.2.a: composed by author; Chart 2.2.a: composed by author; Example 2.2.b: composed by author;
Figure 2.2.d: https://encrypted-tbn0.gstatic.com/images?q=tbn:ANd9GcQ4sDpA4UEHpkRQuq0ZUjNbBbm5eFzk3BUdp6uzaa2ql38_AwPP1w

Figure 2.3.a: https://www.camdencmo.org/wp-content/uploads/2016/11/hipaa_blue-300x159.png

Figure 2.4.a: https://encrypted-tbn0.gstatic.com/images?q=tbn:ANd9GcQnkspAkQmK2U7dmuyFOfWP_3vMDANL_cUkRweKBrHIQ2MjtyW0-w;
Chart 2.4.a: composed by author; Figure 2.4.b: https://www.osha.gov/dcsp/alliances/regional/osha.gif;
Figure 2.4.c: https://www.usp.org/themes/usporg/images/interior_logo.png

Figure 2.5.a: https://explorehealthcareers.org/wp-content/uploads/2016/11/pharmacist.jpg;
Figure 2.5.b: https://explorehealthcareers.org/wp-content/uploads/2017/11/pharmacist-800.jpg;
Figure 2.5.c: https://encrypted-tbn0.gstatic.com/images?q=tbn:ANd9GcRgLVKAvfvhxchUjmDX1iJK5rt0Ce1_owEDF-ANDFuQfF2TVZGjBw

Figure 2.6.a: https://medicalguidelines.msf.org/viewport/EssDr/files/english/16688159/16688160/1/1500887959321/image2017-7-17_16-11-41.png;
Figure 2.6.b:
https://www.google.com/url?q=https://www.shutterstock.com/it/video/clip-34307692-chemist-man-job-pharmacy-store-using-computer&sa=D&ust=1562465758504000&usg=AFQjCNHPv68v6q0tO-y5YhEsFN3U4w2EJg

Figure 2.7.a: https://www.fda.gov/files/Burton-J.-Howard-in-the-Laboratory.jpg; Figure 2.7.b:
https://www.fdli.org/wp-content/uploads/2018/06/fdca.jpg;
Figure 2.7.c: http://ipcblog.org/wp-content/uploads/2011/03/iStock_000008012475XSmall1-childproof-bottle.jpg;
Figure 2.7.d: https://www.drugrehab.org/wp-content/uploads/2017/06/Combat-Methamphetamine-Act_Regulations.png

Chapter 2: *Pharmacy Law and Regulations*

Chapter 3

Sterile & Non-Sterile Compounding

Rx Health Academy

General Information

Nearly 9% of the questions on the PTCB Exam will concern compounding. You need to know the best practices and documentation for both sterile and non-sterile procedures that are outlined in this study guide. If you still have questions about anything here, please consult your instructor.

What you'll learn in this chapter

- Infection control
- Handling and disposal requirements
- Documentation
- Determine product stability
- Selection and use of equipment and supplies
- Sterile compounding processes
- Non-sterile compounding processes

Chapter Outline

3.1 Infection Control for Compounding
3.2 Documentation
3.3 Product Stability
3.4 Equipment and Supplies
3.5 Compounding Risk

3.1 INFECTION CONTROL FOR COMPOUNDING

Product preparation in both sterile and nonsterile compounding requires the use of proper techniques to prevent contamination with bacteria or other potentially harmful substances. The main requirements for prevention of contamination differ for sterile and nonsterile compounding and are listed below. USP 797 and 795 outline the procedural requirements for sterile and nonsterile compounding, respectively.

Sterile

Use appropriate hand washing technique.

Make use of personal protective equipment.

- Gloves
- Gowns
- Feet/shoe covers
- Hair covers (including facial hair)
- Face mask

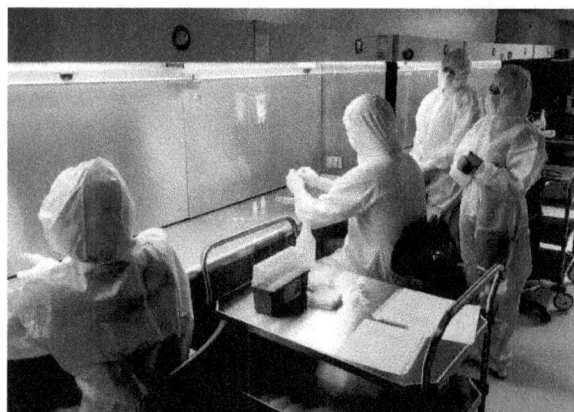

Figure 3.1.a

Clean and disinfect sterile equipment with 70% isopropyl alcohol.

Complete all product preparation and manipulation in the sterile environment.

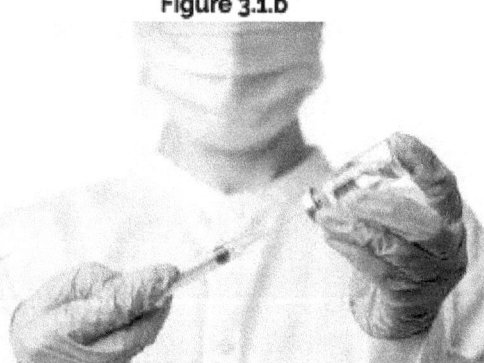

Figure 3.1.b

Non-sterile

Use appropriate hand washing technique.

Use personal protective equipment.

- Gloves
- Face mask
- Apron

Clean and disinfect sterile equipment.

Complete all product preparation and manipulation in the sterile environment.

Handling and Disposal

Just like hazardous substances, pharmaceutical waste has specific handling and disposal criteria that is regulated by state law. For waste that is considered to be hazardous, you should follow the information outlined in the hazardous material section of this text. Pharmaceutical waste must be handled and disposed of in accordance with the *Environmental Protection Agency* (EPA) and must meet all state and federal standards. Characteristics that qualify medication waste as

Chapter 3: *Sterile and Non-Sterile Compounding*

hazardous include corrosiveness, ignitability, reactivity, and toxicity and may include medications such as chemotherapy or immunological drugs.

When preparing medications that may cause hazardous waste, all materials must be stored and manipulated in a negative pressure room to protect the preparer. All waste must be labeled as "hazardous drug waste" and stored in appropriate areas in leak-proof containers. All needles or broken glass should be disposed of in a sharps container.

3.2 DOCUMENTATION

Appropriate documentation is very important for compounded medications and is listed as a requirement under USP 795 and 797. Pharmacies should keep records of all recipes used to make compounded products, as well as specific information for each individual product produced. All compounding records have the same retention requirements as other prescriptions according to state law.

The requirements for each differ and are shown here:

Official Recipe Records

- All ingredients needed to make the compound
- Specific step-by-step instructions for making the compound
- Any calculations needed to prepare the final product
- Information on stability and compatibility
- Any and all labeling requirements for products made from the recipe

Individual Compound Documentation

- Product names and amount/strength of each used including how compound was mixed
- A product specific lot number
- The name of all the people preparing the compound (e.g., technicians and pharmacist who checks it)
- Date of preparation
- Storage requirements
- Beyond-use dating
- Labeling requirements for all prescriptions

3.3 PRODUCT STABILITY

Product compatibility and stability are extremely important for all compounded medications to maintain the integrity and safe use of the medication product. This includes using only compatible substances in a preparation and using the correct beyond-use dating to signify the product is still viable. Just like for any other medication, the beyond-use date is the date when the medication product should not be used. Unlike other medications, however, compounds generally have a much shorter beyond-use date.

The length of stability varies for each specific compound and may be lengthened by using stabilizing agents in the preparation. Consult the product recipe for the specific compound you are preparing. If unknown, the following general rules apply to non-sterile compounds:

Capsules, tablets, other products not made with water—6 months maximum (unless one ingredient has an earlier beyond-use date)

Oral solution with a water base—14 days maximum

Topical solution, ointments, creams—30 days maximum

Sterile compounds have different requirements and generally have even shorter beyond-use dates than non-sterile compounds to ensure sterility of the product.

You should always check the physical product after making the compound to make sure it is stable and compatible. Signs of incompatibility include:
- Formation of a precipitate
- A color change from the original product
- Separation of the ingredients
- Unexpected cloudiness

Note: Not all incompatibility is visible.

3.4 EQUIPMENT AND SUPPLIES

Sterile and nonsterile compounding require the use of appropriate equipment and supplies to prevent contamination with bacteria or other potentially harmful substances. Equipment and supply requirements differ for both sterile and non-sterile compounding.

Sterile Compounding

There are several pieces of equipment used during sterile compounding, all of which are used within a class 5 clean room as outlined in USP 797 and the *International Organization for Standardization* (ISO) environmental standards.

Laminar Flow Hood

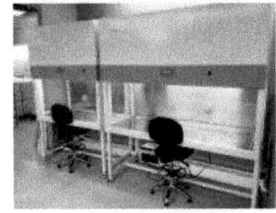

Figure 3.4.a

The laminar flow hood creates an ultra clean environment for sterile compounding by using a *High-Efficiency Particulate Air* (HEPA) filter, which blows air downward and outward from the top and back of the hood, respectively. The air passes through an ultrafine filter before being blown across the workspace, which ensures it is particle-free and reduces the risk of product contamination. The hood needs to be cleaned prior to use and should be inspected on a regular basis to make sure it is working properly.

Drug Containers

Vials—Glass containers with rubber stoppers that contain concentrated medication to be diluted or reconstituted and then diluted as part of a final medication product. Once the plastic lid is removed, vials should be swabbed with 70% isopropyl alcohol prior to any manipulation with a needle. Vials may be single- or multi-use containers.

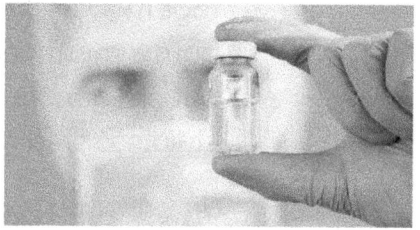

Figure 3.4.b

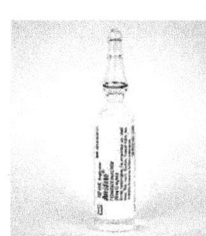

Figure 3.4.c

Ampoules—Glass containers that can be used only once (also referred to as an ampul, ampule, ampulla). Instead of having a rubber stopper for access to its contents, an ampoule must be broken at the neck (the thinnest part of the ampoule) to expose its contents. Because small glass particles may fall into the solution inside, the contents of an ampoule must be withdrawn using a filter needle to prevent contamination. Once the solution is in the syringe, the needle must be changed before any further manipulation can occur.

Syringes—There are three distinct parts of a syringe: the plunger, barrel, and needle. The plunger is used to move medication through the barrel and out the tip through the needle. The internal aspect of the plunger is sterile and should not be touched during product manipulation. All needles should be discarded in a sharps container.

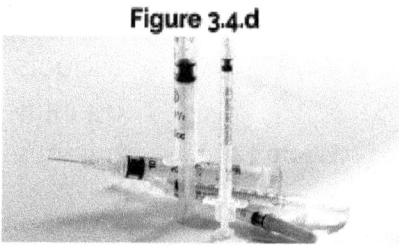

Figure 3.4.d

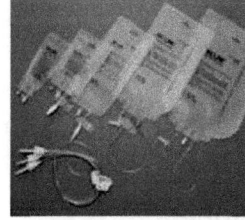

Figure 3.4.e

IV Bags— These are used for diluting and administering medications and come in multiple sizes with various diluents. Each bag contains two distinct ports: one for injecting medication and the other for administration to the patient. Before any manipulation during sterile compounding, the injection port needs to be sterilized with 70% isopropyl alcohol.

Non-sterile Compounding

Because of the variety in the types of nonsterile compounding, the types of supplies needed will depend on the specific preparation. Several key pieces of equipment are common and will be discussed in more detail below. It is important to note that the list is not all-inclusive. For a more comprehensive list, refer to USP 795.

Figure 3.4.f

Mortar and Pestles— Mortars and pestles are used in mixing ingredients together to form various types of liquid-based mixtures. Different mortar

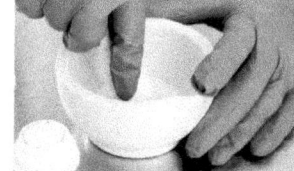

and pestles are ideal for specific products. For example, glass is preferred when making suspensions, oil-based mixtures and porcelain is preferred for blending powders or making wet/dry emulsions.

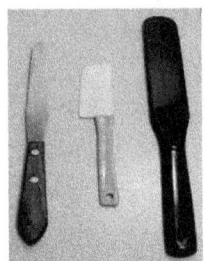

Spatulas—Similar to use when baking, spatulas are used for combining or transferring ingredients and can help to ensure components are evenly mixed together. As well as being utilized to remove a compound from the surfaces of both a mortar and pestle. Spatulas can be made out of multiple types of materials but are generally plastic or rubber in nature, and in some cases stainless steel.

Figure 3.4.h

Figure 3.4.g

Graduated Cylinders—These are used to specifically measure liquids required during product preparation. Always measure from eye level.

Refrigerator and Freezer—All pharmacies are required to have both, and the temperature should be checked regularly and logged in accordance with state law.

Prescription Balance—All pharmacies are required to have a Class A prescription balance that uses brass weights to measure ingredients down to 6 mg increments. The balance uses a counterweight system to determine the specific weight of solid ingredients. Because of the limited specificity, aliquots and geometric dilutions are often needed to measure small quantities. To eliminate this challenge, pharmacies may also use an electric balance, which is more specific and has a digital readout.

Figure 3.4.i

Figure 3.4.j

Product Molds—Capsules, suppositories, lollipops, gummies, troches, etc. all require molds to be prepared adequately in non-sterile compounding. Use the appropriate instructions for each type of mold to ensure the best possible products.

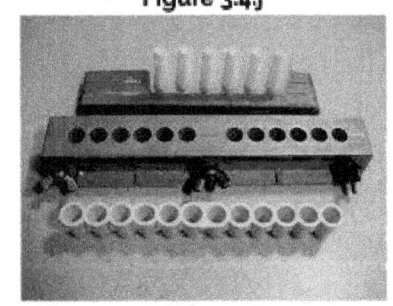

Levigation is the process of grinding an insoluble substance to a fine powder, while wet. The material is introduced into the mill together with water, in which the powdered substance remains suspended, and flows from the mill as a turbid liquid or thin paste, according to the amount of water employed.

Figure 3.4 k

3.5 COMPOUNDING RISK LEVELS

A microbial contamination risk level is an assignment given a particular type of compounded sterile product according to the potential for the introduction of contamination during the compounding process. The assignment of risk level is based on multiple factors including: the type of components used; the environment in which compounding occurs; and the complexity of the compounding process.

USP <797> Microbial Contamination Risk Levels are defined as follows:

Low Risk Level Compounding:
Sterile compounds that are compounded with aseptic manipulations entirely within a ISO Class 5 or better air quality device, usually within an ISO Class 7 environment, using sterile products, components, and devices. Compounded products involve not more than 3 commercially manufactured packages of sterile products and not more than two entries into anyone sterile container or package-e.g, bag or vial. Manipulations are limited to aseptically opening ampules, penetrating disinfected stoppers on vials with sterile needles and sterile syringes

Examples of Low Risk Level Compounding: Reconstitution and transfer of a sterile lgm vial of Cefazolin into one sterile syringe or sterile diluent IV bag.

Medium Risk Level Compounding:
Products are compounded with aseptic manipulations entirely within an ISO Class 5 or better air quality device, usually within an ISO Class 7 environment, using sterile products, components, and devices.

Compounded products are compounded aseptically for multiple individual doses or multiple small doses of sterile products that are pooled together to prepare one sterile compounded product. Compounding process includes complex aseptic manipulations other than single volume transfers using 4 or more sterile ingredients.

Examples of Medium Risk Compounding: A bulk 1gm vial of Vancomycin distributed among several final does, a TPN, a combination of several sterile ingredients into one final dose.

High Risk Level Compounding:

Sterile products compounded from non-sterile ingredients and/or compounded using any non-sterile devices, containers, or equipment. Products prepared from sterile ingredients, containers, devices, or equipment that are exposed to less than ISO Class 5 air.
There is more than a 6-hour delay prior to sterilization of the compounded product.

Examples of High Risk Level Compounding: PCA or epidural compounded from non-sterile powder ingredients. Any ingredient-compounded sterile product relationship involving non-sterile ingredients and/or devices or a compounded sterile product that requires terminal sterilization (filtration, steam, heat, gas, or ionizing radiation).

3.5 OVERVIEW OF PARENTERAL NUTRITION

Parenteral nutrition (PN) is intravenous administration of nutrition, which may include protein, carbohydrate, fat, minerals and electrolytes, vitamins and other trace elements for patients who cannot eat or absorb enough food through tube feeding formula or by mouth to maintain good nutrition status.

Achieving the right nutritional intake in a timely manner can help combat complications and be an important part of a patient's recovery. Parenteral nutrition is sometimes called Total Parenteral Nutrition *(TPN)*.

Parenteral nutrition (PN) provides a means of nourishment for patients in whom oral or enteral nutrition is not possible or practical. Initial formulations consisted of carbohydrates (dextrose), amino acids, vitamins, trace minerals, electrolytes, and water.

- A stable intravenous fat emulsion (IVFE) permitted the combination of all 3 macronutrients in the same admixture (3-in-1 or total nutrient admixture [TNA]).

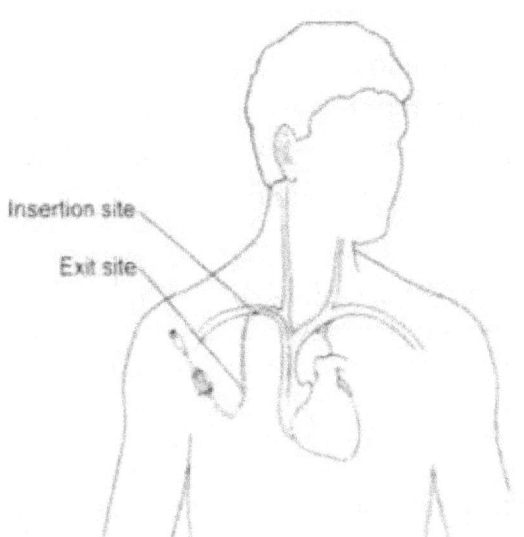

Figure 3.4 l

Chapter 3: *Sterile and Non-Sterile Compounding*

Worksheet 3a: Sterile and Non-Sterile Compounding

1. Which of the following would qualify medication waste as hazardous?
    a) Catalytic, inert, anaerobic, or galvanic
    b) Corrosive, ignitable, reactive, or toxic
    c) Reactive, galvanic, aerobic, or immiscible

2. A requirement for individual compound documentation retention is recording a product's general lot number, True or false?

    True   **False**

3. The length of stability varies for each specific compound and may be lengthened by using _____ in the preparation.

4. List two differences and similarities in the Venn diagram for the following terms: <u>vials</u> and <u>ampoules</u>

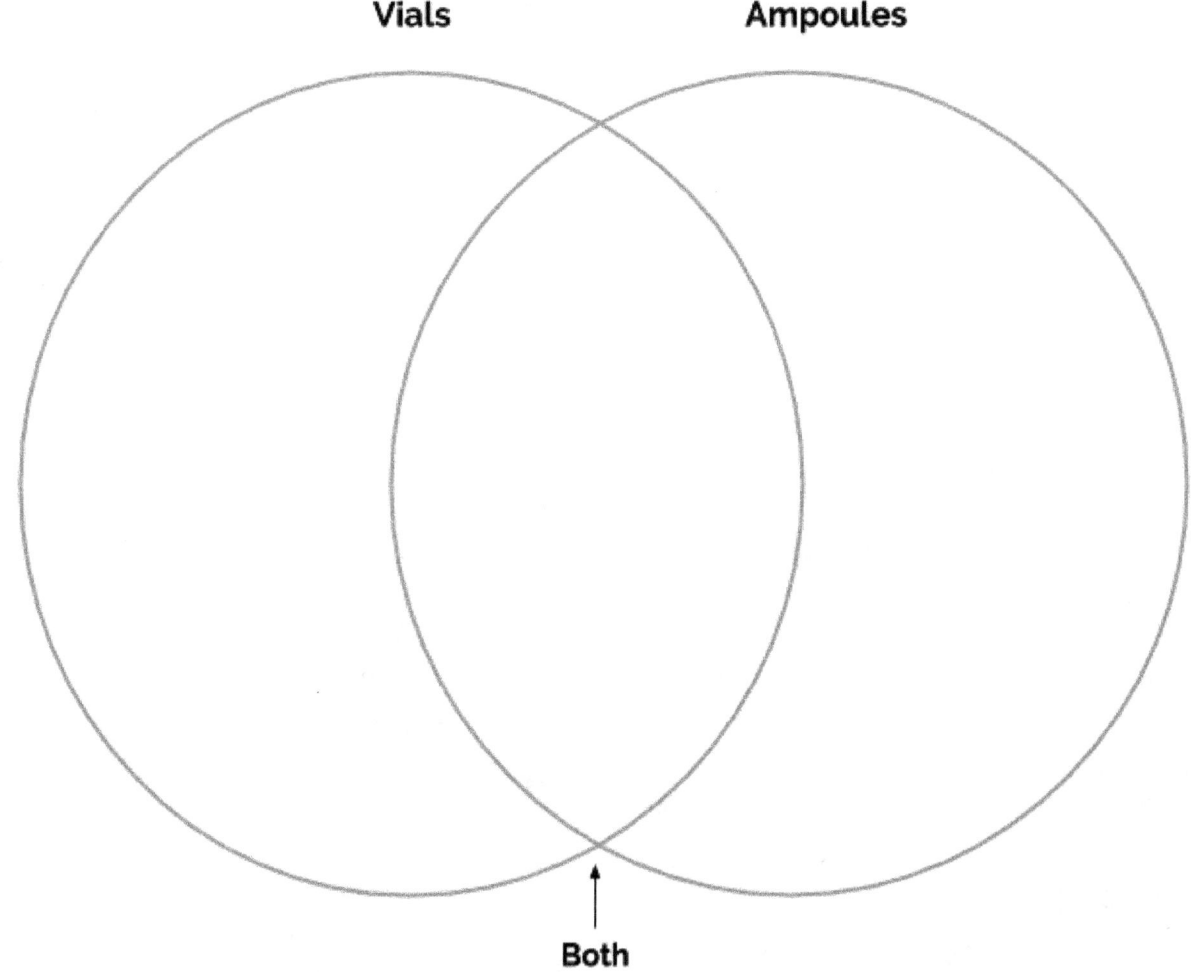

Both

Worksheet 3b: Sterile and Non-Sterile Compounding

5. List the preferred <u>mortar and pestle</u> to match the type of compound

   Suspensions : _____

   Powders or wet/dry emulsions :

6. Which drug does <u>NOT</u> require a mold to be prepared while conducting non-sterile compounding?
   a) promethazine
   b) Airborne Vitamin C
   c) clotrimazole
   d) Dimetapp

Chapter 3: *Sterile and Non-Sterile Compounding*

Sterile and Non-Sterile Compounding Quiz

1. Which of the following equipment is NOT used in non-sterile compounding procedures?
    a) Graduated cylinder
    b) Mortar and pestle
    c) Laminar flow hood

2. Pharmacy personnel use various techniques when compounding preparations. Which of the following statements best describes levigation?
    a) The process of grinding a powder through the incorporation of a liquid
    b) The process of reducing a particle's size by incorporating a substance in which that particle is soluble
    c) The process of reducing the particle size of an ingredient by grinding it into a powder

3. Compounded sterile preparations are categorized by risk levels. Which of the following does NOT describe a low-risk level
    a) Compounded using aseptic manipulations in an ISO Class 5 environment
    b) Sterile components, antimicrobial-free CSPs, and sterile surfaces exposed to air quality worse than an ISO Class 5
    c) Compounding involving no more than three commercially available products and no more than two entries into any sterile container or bag.

4. Laminar flow hoods should be disinfected with what type of solution?
    a) Betadine solution
    b) 70% isopropyl alcohol
    c) Antibacterial soap

5. Which is the appropriate beyond use date (BUD) for an oral suspension that does not have stability information on the product label?
    a) BUD no later than 30 days
    b) BUD no later than 6 months or equal to the earliest expiration date of any active pharmaceutical ingredient
    c) BUD no later than 14 days from the reconstitution date

6. Which of the following units are used when interpreting an expression of a percentage (e.g., 10%)?
    a) mg/mL
    b) mg/L
    c) g/mL

Chapter 3: *Sterile and Non-Sterile Compounding*

7. Which way does air flow in a horizontal laminar flow hood?
    a) From back to front
    b) From top to bottom
    c) From side to side

8. Which of the following devices should be calibrated prior to use?
    a) Class A prescription balance
    b) Graduated cylinder
    c) Laminar fluid hood

9. A filter needle is required when withdrawing solution from which of these?
    a) a vial
    b) an IV bag
    c) an ampule

10. 3-in-1 TPN admixtures allow for simultaneous infusion of what ingredients?
    a) Fats, multivitamins, and dextrose
    b) Dextrose, amino acids, and fats
    c) Protein, sugar, and fats

Chapter 3: *Sterile and Non-Sterile Compounding*

Quiz: Study Guide

Question Number	Section Reference
1	3.4
2	3.4
3	3.5
4	3.1
5	3.3
6	3.4
7	3.4
8	3.4
9	3.4
10	3.6

Chapter References

Figure 3.1.a: https://news.vcu.edu/image/9465/90x60;
Figure 3.1.b: https://encrypted-tbn0.gstatic.com/images?q=tbn:ANd9GcSKd6ZsWyMMw8xQdmUdqZzfpyFs-YHwD4Sy4n9TomK51p2EfGgZwA;

Figure 3.4.a: http://www.healthmark.ca/DATA/PRODUIT/283_1_1.jpg;
Figure 3.4.b: https://www.rx3pharmacy.com/wp-content/uploads/2018/03/sterile2.jpg;
Figure 3.4.c: https://d2ch1jyy91788s.cloudfront.net/buyemp/images/product/437a-250_250.jpg;
Figure 3.4.d: http://www.pyramidspharmacy.com/img/sterile_banner.jpg; Figure 3.4.e: http://www.healthmark.ca/DATA/PRODUIT/88_1_1.jpg;
Figure 3.4.f: https://sandsrx.com/wp-content/uploads/2014/04/hands_morter-c9b3553a43c1188441bde6a748124a10.jpg;
Figure 3.4.g: https://basicmedicalkey.com/wp-content/uploads/2016/06/image01133-1.jpeg;
Figure 3.4.h: https://basicmedicalkey.com/wp-content/uploads/2016/06/image01138-4.jpeg;
Figure 3.4.i: http://store.apothecaryproducts.com/media/catalog/product/cache/1/image/9df78eab33525d08d6e5fb8d27136e95/2/4/24028_6.jpg;
Figure 3.4.j: https://encrypted-tbn0.gstatic.com/images?q=tbn:ANd9GcTNDeTxYMT7nofYDZ68Wj2fcBSxmc2DLUr8JXJVXa1fW-e6clc0
Figure 3.4 k: https://www.google.com/imgres?imgurl=https%3A%2F%2Fi.ytimg.com%2Fvi%2FG4vzxzk7Cqg%2Fmaxresdefault.jpg
Figure 3.4 l: http://www.nutritioncare.org/about_clinical_nutrition/what_is_parenteral_nutrition/

Chapter 4

Medication Safety

Rx Health Academy

General Information

Safety when dispensing medicine is of utmost importance, and over 12% of the questions on the PTCB Exam are devoted to this subject. The basics of medication safety are outlined below, but, if you need more information, be sure to access online sources, textbook, or instructor for help.

What you'll learn in this chapter

- Error prevention strategies for data entry
- Patient package insert and medication guide requirements
- Identify issues that require pharmacist intervention
- Look-alike/sound-alike medications
- High-alert/risk medications
- Common safety strategies

Chapter Outline

4.1 Medication Errors and Error Prevention
4.2 Information for the Patient
4.3 Specific Recommendations
4.4 Similar Medications
4.5 Common Safety Strategies

4.1 Medication Errors and Error Prevention

Medication errors are broadly defined by the National Coordinating Council for Medication Error Reporting and Prevention (NCC MERP) as "…any preventable event that may cause or lead to inappropriate medication use or patient harm." An example of an event that would not be considered a medication error is a severe allergic reaction that had not been previously reported and could not be reasonably predicted based on patient and medication characteristics. However, an allergic reaction previously reported by the patient that was overlooked would be considered a medication error since it could have been prevented through proper use of available information.

Medication Errors

Common types of medication errors are: prescribing, omission, wrong-time, unauthorized drug, improper dose, wrong dosage form, wrong drug preparation, wrong administration technique, deteriorated drug, monitoring and adherence errors along with miscellaneous error not falling into any of these categories. See Table 4.1.a.: Examples of Medication Errors by Type.

Examples of Medication Errors by Type — Table 4.1.a

Medication Error Type	Examples
Prescribing Error	- Provider prescribes a medication to which a patient has a severe allergy - Prescription/medication order is illegible - Dosing is incorrect for kidney function
Omission Error	- Nurse cannot locate drug product and patient misses entire dose - Medication requires prior authorization from insurance and patient does not receive medication
Wrong Time Error	- Nurse cannot locate drug product and drug administration is delayed - Medication requires prior authorization from insurance and patient experiences a delay in obtaining medication
Unauthorized Drug Error	- An automated dispensing machine is stocked with the incorrect drug product and patient receives the incorrect medication - A prescription is filled with the incorrect medication, but labeled for the prescribed drug
Improper Dose Error	- An automated dispensing machine is stocked with the incorrect dose and patient receives the incorrect dose - A prescription is filled with the incorrect dose but labeled for the

	prescribed dose
Wrong Dosage Form Error	• A suppository is dispensed when a capsule was ordered • A cream is dispensed in place of an ointment
Wrong Drug Preparation Error	• Incorrect diluent used in compounding parenteral product • Incorrect ratio of ingredients added to compounded liquid medication
Deteriorated Drug Error	• A patient purchases an expired bottle of over-the-counter medication • A pharmacy dispenses tablets that have been stored at a temperature outside the appropriate range
Monitoring Error	• A medication requires lab monitoring but pharmacy depenses without labs
Adherence Error	• Patient does not take the full course of antibiotics because he/she is feeling better • Patient takes daily blood pressure medications only every other day for cost saving

Causes of Medication Errors

Medication errors can occur at any step of the medication use process, ranging from prescribing and transcribing to dispensing and administering. Even after a medication has been used, if it is not appropriately monitored, an error may occur. It is important to identify the source of a medication error to avoid future problems; identifying a singular source may be challenging, however, as medication errors are often multifactorial.

Knowledge vs. Performance Errors

Knowledge and performance deficits are two distinct reasons medication errors may occur. In the case of a pharmacy employee, if a person does not have the necessary training to complete a task, this would be considered a *knowledge deficit*. On the other hand, if a person has sufficient knowledge to complete a task but does not appropriately apply that knowledge, is distracted by other aspects of the job, or is tired and therefore less alert while working, these would be considered *performance deficits*.

Persons Responsible for Errors

Everyone who plays a role in a patient's care—including the patient—is responsible for identifying and preventing medication errors. Thinking about the medication use process, prescribers must choose the correct drug, dose, route, frequency, and quantity. Then, to get a prescription from the prescriber to the patient may require several steps involving nurses, pharmacy personnel, and family members. The pharmacy team is responsible for identifying potential transcribing errors and reviewing the patient's complete medication regimen before dispensing a new medication. Medication administration may be the responsibility of a nurse, family member, or the patient and should provide an additional checkpoint to ensure that the correct patient is receiving the correct drug at the correct time. Finally, a monitoring plan must be employed to ensure long-term safety and effectiveness.

Data Entry Error Prevention

Data entry and order transcribing are of the utmost importance in the medication use process, and these tasks are often handled by pharmacy technicians. To minimize the potential for medication errors, the "5 Rights" of medication use (i.e., ensuring that the right medication and right dose are given to the right patient at the right time via the right route) should always be considered when performing data entry.

4.2 INFORMATION FOR THE PATIENT

Pharmacy personnel provide medication information to patients in a number of different ways. Specific paperwork and precautions are discussed here.

Package Insert and Medication Guide Requirements

Patient package inserts and medication guides accompany those medications with potential significant risks. Both guidance documents contain information about these risks; patient *package inserts* typically discuss benefits and risks of a particular medication, while *medication guides* provide guidance on how to minimize the risk of experiencing a serious adverse drug event.

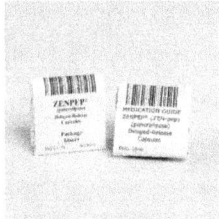

Figure 4.1.a   Figure 4.1.b

Special Directions and Precautions

Some high-risk medications require patients or pharmacies to enroll in a registry and/or participate in ongoing monitoring. Knowing for which drugs these special precautions are most often taken in your pharmacy will help you anticipate patient questions and appropriately refer the patient for pharmacist counseling.

Pharmacist Intervention

A pharmacist should always be available in the pharmacy in case of questions or concerns. Developing a collaborative relationship and knowing when to consult your pharmacist colleagues will help you be successful as a pharmacy technician.

4.3 SPECIFIC RECOMMENDATIONS

Pharmacists are to conduct *drug utilization reviews* (DURs) prior to dispensing a new medication or refilling and existing order. The DUR should include a comprehensive review of the patient's prescription and over-the-counter (OTC) medications, with a special focus on drug-drug interactions and potential adverse drug events (ADEs). Pharmacists should be consulted in case patients have questions or concerns about any of their medications (including OTCs) or if drug misuse or abuse is suspected.

Therapeutic Substitution

Therapeutic substitution allows for a medication to be switched to a different medication in the same drug class (though not the same drug) without first checking with the prescriber. This practice is especially common in hospitals and federal facilities, in which cases analyses of safety, effectiveness, and cost often determine which limited supply of drugs will be maintained on site. It is important to note that therapeutic substitution is different than generic substitution, which occurs when the generic version of a drug is substituted for the brand name drug (e.g., "Zoloft" is prescribed but "sertraline" [generic for Zoloft] is dispensed).

Missed Dose

Identifying underlying causes of missed doses can help avoid treatment failures and adverse outcomes moving forward. Much like medication errors, the cause of a missed dose may be multifactorial. Monitoring a patient's medication profile for lapsed refills can help identify the problem, and pharmacist counseling on the importance of medication adherence and potential adherence strategies can help get patients and caregivers back on track.

Misuse

Medication misuse—whether intentional or unintentional—is a public health crisis. Medication misuse may occur in a number of different ways; for example, a person may take someone else's sertraline to self-medicate his or her depression, a person may take lorazepam more often than prescribed because of increasing anxiety, or a person may intentionally take oxycodone in an effort to "get high." Regardless of the cause or intent, pharmacy personnel should be vigilant regarding fraudulent prescriptions and changes in patient behavior to help identify cases of misuse and abuse.

4.4 SIMILAR MEDICATIONS

Similar medications are a serious safety concern and a common cause of medication errors. Just because two medications' names look or sound alike does not mean they can be used interchangeably. Moreover, errors in communication or drug selection can have potentially fatal consequences.

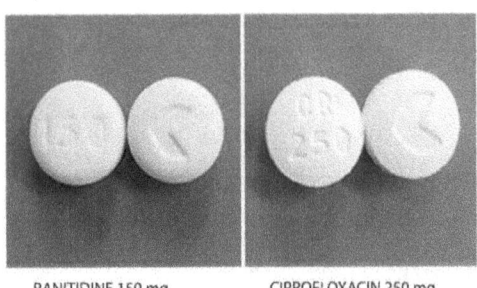

Figure 4.4.a

Look-Alike Medications

For drugs that look like other drugs, pharmacy technicians should always double-check the drug name and strength. For example, observe the similarities between the 150mg ranitidine (antacid/antihistamine) and 250mg ciprofloxacin (antibiotic) tablets.

Sound-Alike Medications

As in the case of look-alike drugs, pharmacy technicians should always double-check the drug name and strength of sound-alike drugs. Consider the example of hydralazine (an antihypertensive) and hydroxyzine (an antihistamine). These drugs look the same except for the middle three letters. Therefore, on the bottle and when communicating the drug name in writing, those different letters will be capitalized to draw the reader's eye to the potential discrepancy (e.g., hydrALAzine vs. hydrOXYzine). Simply asking the person speaking to spell the drug name can help clarify that the correct drug is being discussed.

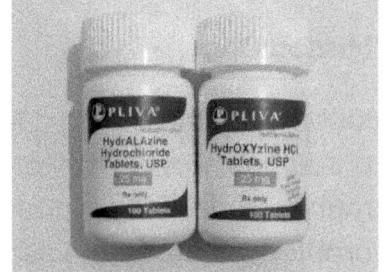

Figure 4.4.b

High-Alert and High-Risk Medications

High-alert and *high-risk medications* are those medications that are more likely to cause harm to a patient if used incorrectly or in error. For example, the blood-thinning drug warfarin has the potential to cause significant bleeding in the case of a drug overdose, drug interaction, or drug monitoring error. The *Institute for Safe Medication Practices* (ISMP) is the primary resource for identifying high-alert medications like warfarin.

4.5 COMMON SAFETY STRATEGIES

Different pharmacies use different safety strategies to reduce the potential for medication errors. It is important to understand your employer's safety-related processes and procedures.

Notation Strategies

Abbreviations should be avoided whenever possible. For example, "QD" should be written out as "once a day" or "daily" to avoid confusion with QID (four times a day) or QOD (every other day). In the busy work environment, abbreviations may seem faster or easier to use, but spelling out what you mean will save time—and prevent errors—in the long run. Likewise, for whole numbers, do not use "trailing zeros," as in the case of 5.0; instead, simply write the whole number (5) and add units. Of note, a zero should be added before a decimal point in the case of 0.5 mg or 0.75 mL to minimize the risk of overdose. Tall man lettering (discussed above) is another notation strategy to use in the case of look-alike and sound-alike medications such as AlprazOLam and lorazepam. Refer to Table 4.5.a for meanings of common abbreviations.

Chapter 4: *Medication Safety*

Table 4.5.a

	Abbreviation	Meaning	Abbreviation	Meaning
Route of Administration	a.d.	right ear	top.	topically, locally
	a.s., a.l.	left ear	p.r.	rectally, into the rectum
	a.u.	each ear	p.v.	vaginally, into the vagina
	o.d.	right eye	i.m., IM	intramuscular
	o.s., o.l.	left eye	i.v., IV	intravenous
	o.u.	each eye	i.v.p., IVP	intravenous push
	p.o.	by mouth	IVPB	intravenous piggyback
	S.L.	sublingually, under the tongue	SC, subc, subq	subcutaneously
	per neb	by nebulizer		
Dosage Form	tab.	tablet	syr.	syrup
	cap	capsule	liq.	liquid
	SR, XR, XL	slow/extended release	supp.	suppository
	sol	solution	crm	cream
	susp	suspension	ung., oint	ointment
Timing of Administration	q.d.	every day	prn	as needed
	bid	twice a day	a.c.	before food, before meals
	tid	three times a day	p.c.	after food, after meals
	qid	four times a day	stat.	immediately
	a.m.	morning	q__h	every__ hour(s)
	p.m.	afternoon or evening	qod	every other day
	h.s.	at bedtime		
Measurement	ī, īī	one, two, etc.	mcg., µg	microgram
	ss	one-half	mg.	milligram
	gtt.	drop	g., G., gm.	gram
	ml., mL	milliliter, millilitre	mEq.	milliequivalent
	tsp.	teaspoon (= 5 mL)	a.a. or aa	of each
	tbsp.	tablespoon (= 15 ml)	ad	to, up to
	fl. oz.	fluid ounce (= 30 mL)	aq. ad	add water up to
	l, L	liter/Litre	qs, q.s. ad	add sufficient quantity to make
Other	UTD	as directed	c, w/	with
	NR, ø	no refill	s̄, w/o	without

Worksheet 4a: Medication Safety

1. Write the medication error for each example.

    a) Patient takes daily blood pressure medications only every other day for cost saving.

    _____

    b) An automated dispensing machine is stocked with the incorrect dose and patient receives the incorrect dose.

    _____

    c) An automated dispensing machine is stocked with the incorrect dose and patient receives the incorrect dose.

    _____

    d) A suppository is dispensed when a capsule was ordered.

    _____

    e) Incorrect ratio of ingredients added to compounded liquid medication.

    _____

2. In a patient's care regimen, the people responsible for preventing medication errors are: a nurse, pharmacy team, _____, and the patient.

3. Therapeutic substitution allows for a medication to be switched to a different medication in the same drug class by checking with the prescriber first. True or false?

    True   **False**

4. What is the most common way to avoid medication error with sound alike medications? What characteristics should you double check with look alike medications?

    _____

    _____

5. The ISMP is a nonprofit organization that specializes in which of the following?
    a) Sterile and non-sterile compounding
    b) Regulation of controlled substances
    c) Data entry software
    d) Safe medication practices

Chapter 4: *Medication Safety*

Worksheet 4a: Medication Safety

6. Complete the Venn diagram for the following terms:

    package inserts and medication guides

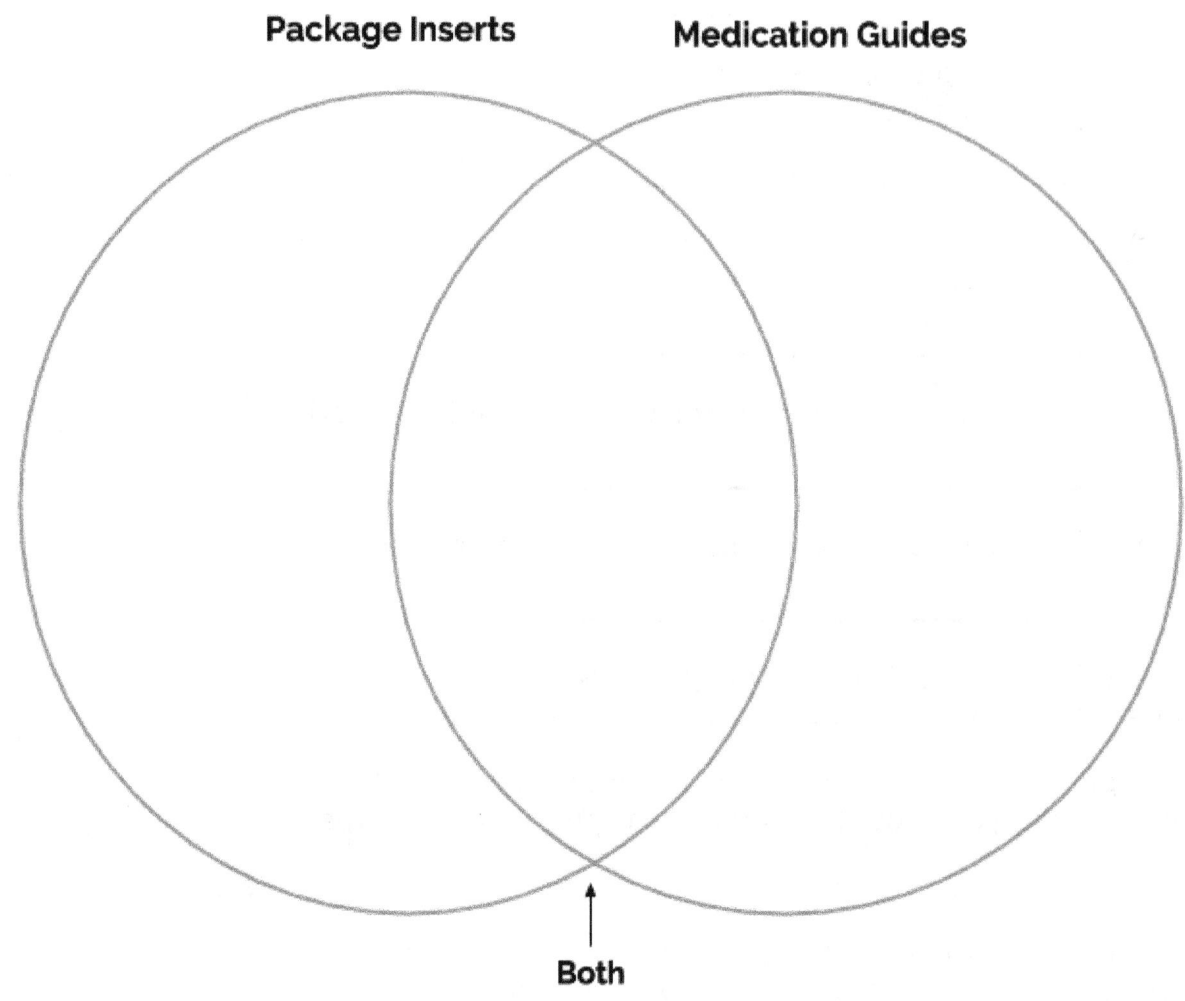

7. Match the meaning to the following abbreviations.

    <u>top</u>   <u>o.u.</u>   <u>p.c.</u>   <u>mEq.</u>   <u>crm</u>   <u>prn</u>   <u>h.s.</u>   <u>gtt.</u>   <u>sol</u>   <u>aa</u>

    each eye   milliequivalent   topically   after food   at bedtime   solution

    drop   of each   cream   as needed

Chapter 4: *Medication Safety*

Medication Safety Quiz

1. A medication error may be the result of the wrong _____.
    a) Prescriber
    b) Dosage form
    c) Day's supply
    d) All of the above

2. The drugs Zyrtec 10 mg and Zoloft 10 mg are examples of _____.
    a) Over-the-counter (OTC) medications
    b) Look-alike names
    c) Therapeutic substitutions
    d) Tall man lettering

3. Pharmacy technicians interpreting unclear prescriptions should _____.
    a) Not request assistance and just fill the prescription
    b) Check with the pharmacist
    c) Call the doctor
    d) All of the above

4. "AlprazOLam" is an example of a medicine with _____.
    a) Tall man lettering
    b) A look-alike/sound-alike name
    c) A drug utilization review
    d) HIPAA

5. Which of the following is an example of a knowledge deficit?
    a) Personnel are distracted by noise.
    b) An employee comes into work with a fever and a cough.
    c) The employee lacks training.
    d) The employee is going through a difficult time in his/her personal life.

6. Which of the following is an example of an error caused by the prescriber?
    a) Illegible handwriting
    b) Family members bringing in medications for the patient without staff approval
    c) Borrowing medications from another patient
    d) Labeling error

7. True or False: Abuse and/or misuse of medications may be unintentional or intentional.

8. Error prevention strategies in the pharmacy setting include
   a) Separating the inventory of medications with similar names
   b) Avoiding the use of error-prone abbreviations
   c) Organizing medications by formulation
   d) All of the above

9. True or False: Medication guides contain FDA-approved information that can help patients avoid serious adverse effects.

10. Medication Errors can occur for many reasons. Which of the following is a reason why a patient may miss or skip a dose?
    a) The patient forgot to take the medication
    b) The patient's caregiver did not give the medication to the patient
    c) The patient ran out of the medication
    d) All of the above

Chapter 4: *Medication Safety*

Quiz: Study Guide

Question Number	Section Reference
1	4.1
2	4.3
3	4.2
4	4.5
5	4.2
6	4.1
7	4.1
8	4.4
9	4.5
10	4.1

Chapter References

Table 4.1.a: chart composed by author

Figure 4.2.a: https://www.flottmanco.com/wp-content/uploads/2018/01/featured-435x435.jpg;
Figure 4.2.b: http://platinumpress.com/wp-content/uploads/2014/01/medication_guide_rev.jpg;

Figure 4.4.a: https://i.cbc.ca/1.2926640.1421868736!/fileImage/httpImage/image.png_gen/derivatives/original_780/lookalike-pills.png;
Figure 4.4.b: https://news.hofstra.edu/wp-content/uploads/2018/05/news-hotizons-spring18-schroeder-fig2.jpg:

Chapter 5

Pharmacy Quality Assurance

Rx Health Academy

General Information

"Everybody makes mistakes." You've heard this before and it's certainly true, even in a pharmacy. *However*, when dealing with people's health, a mistake can be extremely dangerous, so the goal of good pharmacy workers is to identify and acknowledge errors and *reduce* their occurrence. Following is information to help you do your part in this reduction as a pharmacy technician.

What you'll learn in this chapter

- Quality assurance practices for medication and inventory control systems
- Infection control procedures and documentation
- Risk management guidelines and regulations
- Communication channels necessary to ensure appropriate follow-up and problem resolution
- Productivity, efficiency, and customer satisfaction measures

Chapter Outline

5.1 Quality Assurance Practices
5.2 Education Standards and Information Technology
5.3 Infection Control for Quality Assurance

5.1 QUALITY ASSURANCE PRACTICES

Quality assurance practices, as the name suggests, are put in place to ensure high quality and safety during all pharmacy operations. The practices contain the prevention, identification, and change implementation concerning all processes related to pharmacy practice that may be unsafe or ineffective. Generally, these practices are centered on medication use and inventory. Quality assurance should be practiced by all pharmacy personnel.

Continuous Quality Improvement (CQI)

CQI is a set of methods to help improve pharmacy practices and should occur on a regular and continual basis. The methods should help pharmacy personnel find, assess, and document issues, then implement changes to improve the process. Although the process may differ slightly from pharmacy to pharmacy, several steps should take place to ensure successful CQI:

1. Evaluate the medication use process.
2. Identify and document medication errors within specific categories.
3. Create an environment to support medication error reporting.
    - Focus on improvement.
    - Enable anonymous reporting.
    - Don't focus on punishment.
4. Develop interventions to improve the process and prevent errors from occuring.

Prevention Strategies

The best way to deal with medication errors is to prevent them from occurring in the first place. Many practices can be implemented, used by themselves or in combination, to reduce the chances of a medication error and, if it does occur, to reduce the likelihood that it will reach the patient.

Fail-safes and Constraints

Fail-safes and *constraints* represent system changes that prevent errors from making it through part of the medication use process. An example would be the computer system not letting pharmacy personnel fill a prescription and print out a label without putting all the necessary information on the label first.

Forcing Functions

Forcing functions are programmed stops in the medication use process that "force" you to manually bypass them by providing some sort of verification. An example of this would be a pharmacist using a password to acknowledge identity when verifying a prescription.

Automation and Computerization

Improvements in technology have lead to an increasing use of automation and computerization in many pharmacies. This can help reduce errors by removing the human factor from various processes. Typically, automation is involved in filling prescriptions or checking for drug interactions between a patient's various medications.

Standardization

Standardization refers to using a consistent method to do something that can help reduce errors by going through the same, stepwise process each time the procedure is done. An example of this would be a pharmacist verifying information on a prescription. If they work in the same order every time, they are much more likely to find any errors.

Redundancies, Reminders, and Checklists

Following checklists and using redundancy can help eradicate the human error factor during pharmacy operations. Checkpoints along the way, with reminders and notifications, help to improve the accuracy of a procedure like filling a prescription or restocking an automated medicine cabinet. Having redundancies in the process will also help you double-check your work to ensure medication and workplace safety.

5.2 EDUCATION STANDARDS AND INFORMATION TECHNOLOGY

These describe a certain level of skill in understanding of the practice of pharmacy. They can include state and federal laws, additional training for the type of pharmacy you work in, and infection-control procedures. Often, pharmacy personnel need to complete *continuing education* (CE) hours annually to ensure they meet the appropriate educational standards.

Policies and Procedures

Policies and procedures are a set of rules to follow when performing pharmacy operations. They dictate everything from workflow to job responsibilities of members of the pharmacy workforce. CQI helps to reinforce policies and can help improve on the standards of practice. This can occur through two steps. The first is *quality control*, which is related to the identification of areas that might need improvement. This is followed by *quality assurance*, which is a longitudinal process that is continuous and focuses on more broad, systemic processes.

Calibration of Instruments

All of the instruments used in the pharmacy are required to be very accurate to ensure the purest quality and the best possible product. To maintain the accuracy of the instruments, they need regular cleaning and maintenance. This often includes calibration where a standard is used to make minor modifications to the measurements the device makes so that it meets the highest possible standards of accuracy. An example of this would be a scale used to measure ingredients for a compound or the volume dispensed in an automatic TPN compounding machine.

Employee Management

In any pharmacy operation, employee management is perhaps the most important aspect of quality control. This starts with hiring the right people and making schedules to match the demands of the work environment. Being understaffed can create an environment conducive to errors. Proper training in multiple aspects or areas of the pharmacy will ensure everyone understands what needs to be done to ensure quality. Having a standardized workflow can also help by using a process that everyone can learn and follow. This will improve consistency and reduce the chance of errors.

National Drug Code (NDC)

As mentioned in Chapter 2, the *NDC* consists of three sets of numbers that help identify the drugs manufacturer (first set of digits), the medication name (middle set of digits), and the package size (last set of digits). No two drugs have the same NDC code. A good way to think about it is that the NDC code is that individual product's fingerprint. Matching an NDC code to the product selected during the prescription processing procedure can help eliminate human error in filling prescriptions.

Bar Codes

Similar to NDC codes, each drug's *barcode* is also unique and can be used to verify that the correct product is chosen. It is impossible to do this with the naked eye. Instead, a scanner may be used to scan the individual drug product into the system and to verify the correct drug is chosen in the filling process.

Data Entry

The process of *data entry* is something that can be difficult to standardize or use technology to support. Rather this is often a completely manual process. Due to the potential for human error, quality assurance needs to be at the forefront of pharmacy procedures. Constantly evaluating ways to improve the accuracy of data entry such as using a multiple verification process can improve patient safety.

5.3 INFECTION CONTROL FOR QUALITY ASSURANCE

Infection control is incredibly important to protect the safety of pharmacy personnel, drug products, and the patients that the pharmacy serves. Using the proper procedures will help prevent the spread of infections and are required by state and federal pharmacy laws. Specific procedures such as the appropriate order to don PPE need to be followed and all training and infection-control policies and procedures need to be appropriately documented.

Personal Health and Hygiene

All pharmacy personnel have the potential to spread illness and infection through direct or indirect contact with medications and patients. It is incredibly important for everyone to maintain proper personal hygiene to reduce the risk of infecting patients or contaminating drug products. This includes not working when sick and being clean and well-kept when working in the pharmacy.

Hand Washing

Hand washing is one of the easiest, yet most important, aspects of infection control. Always wash your hands prior to any compounding procedure or pharmacy process that involves direct contact with the drug product. This includes washing your hands prior to donning PPE in accordance with USP 795 and 797.

Personal Protective Equipment (PPE)

As previously mentioned in Chapter 2, *PPE* is required for all compounding procedures and differs based on the type of compounding and the drug products being compounded.

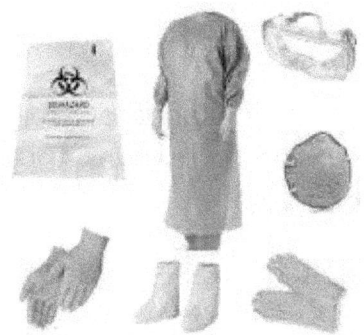

When using PPE, it is important to follow a specific order to reduce the potential of contamination. In general, you should work from "dirtiest" to "cleanest" parts of the PPE attire. For example, you wouldn't put shoe covers on after putting on your sterile gloves. Follow the general order listed here and make sure to check the procedures outlined by your specific pharmacy.

1. Remove outer garments, jewelry, makeup, artificial nails, piercings, etc. before putting on any PPE.
2. Start with shoe and hair covers including any facial hair.
3. Put on a face mask or face shield.
4. Wash your hands with appropriate hand washing technique, from hand to elbow, for at least 30 seconds.
5. Use a compounding specific gown.
6. Don sterile gloves and use alcohol to continue to sterile your gloved hands between drug products.

For more details, see our compounding study guide and refer to the procedures outlined in USP 795 and 797.

Needle Recapping

Many compounding procedures require the use of needles for product manipulation or preparation. After using a needle, it should never be recapped because doing so puts you at an increased risk for a needle stick. Instead, you should place the needle, facing downward, into an appropriate disposal location, such as a sharps container.

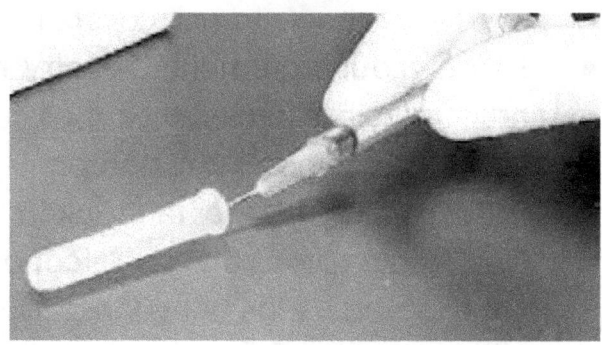

Chapter 5: *Pharmacy Quality Assurance*

Worksheet 5: Pharmacy Quality Assurance

1. Quality assurance practices contain the prevention, identification, and _____ concerning all processes related to pharmacy practice that may be unsafe or ineffective.

2. Fill in the following diagram to indicate each step that encourages successful CQI

   ☐ → ☐ → ☐ → ☐

3. The term <u>quality control</u> is defined as:

   _____

4. The NDC code of any product is that individual product's fingerprint. True or false?

   True   **False**

5. The process of _____ is something that can be difficult to standardize or use technology to support. Due to the potential for human error during manual input, quality assurance needs to be at the forefront of pharmacy procedures.

6. Match the number to each step in chronological order for standard PPE procedure.

   - Use a compounding specific gown.
   - Start with shoe and hair covers including any facial hair.
   - Remove outer garments, jewelry, makeup, artificial nails, piercings, etc. before putting on any PPE.
   - Wash your hands with appropriate hand washing technique.
   - Put on a face mask or face shield.
   - Don sterile gloves and use alcohol to continue to sterile your gloved hands between drug products.

   ① ② ③ ④ ⑤ ⑥

7. In some cases, it is appropriate to recap needles during product preparation. True or false?

   True   **False**

Chapter 5: *Pharmacy Quality Assurance*

Pharmacy Quality Assurance Quiz

1. Which of the following is NOT a preventative strategy used to reduce medication errors?
    a) Providing a notation before overriding a high-alert medication
    b) The use of auxiliary labels to provide warnings and alerts
    c) Inadequate or incorrect packaging, labeling, or directions
    d) The use of e-prescribing or CPOE to avoid transcription or misinterpretation errors

2. Which organization oversees the National Medication Errors Reporting Program (MERP)?
    a) ISMP
    b) TJC
    c) State Board of Pharmacy
    d) USP

3. Proper hand-washing technique requires washing the hand from the forearm to the _____.
    a) Elbow
    b) Shoulder
    c) Neck
    d) Face

4. Which of the following is NOT a process used in continuous quality improvement programs?
    a) Detect and document
    b) Evaluate
    c) Report
    d) pursue

5. What should the preparer do with his or her needle and syringe following the compounding of a non hazardous, sterile prescription?
    a) Recap it, and toss it into the sharps container.
    b) Do not recap it; toss it in the sharps container.
    c) Remove the needle, and toss it into the sharps container.
    d) Use the Luer Lock, and toss it into the waste receptacle.

Chapter 5: *Pharmacy Quality Assurance*

6. A recall was issued by the FDA for medication "X." Who should contact the patient to let him
    know that his medication has been recalled?
    a) FDA
    b) Pharmacy
    c) Manufacturer
    d) Prescriber

7. What should be removed before entering the cleanroom or sterile compounding area?
    a) Outer garments
    b) Cosmetics
    c) Jewelry
    d) All of the above

8. The identification of errors that require change due to inconsistencies is called _____.
    a) Continuous quality improvement
    b) Quality assurance
    c) Quality control
    d) Quality

9. What is the minimum amount of time that your hands should be washed before you participate in preparing sterile compounding procedures?
    a) 30 seconds
    b) 45 seconds
    c) 60 seconds
    d) 120 seconds

10. What items should be placed into a sharps container?
    a) Syringes and needles
    b) Vials
    c) Hazardous waste
    d) Gloves

Chapter 5: *Pharmacy Quality Assurance*

Quiz: Study Guide

Question Number	Section Reference
1	5.1
2	4.1
3	5.1
4	5.1
5	5.3
6	2.4
7	5.3
8	5.1
9	5.3
10	3.1, 5.3

Chapter 6

Pharmacy Math

Rx Health Academy

General Information

In addition to interpreting abbreviations, pharmacy technicians must also how to perform calculations in order to input a day's supply, determine the dose to administer based on the dose and hand, or adjust refills.

What you'll learn in this chapter

- Pharmacy Calculations for Pharmacy Technicians.
- Use mental math to solving calculations

Chapter Outline

6.1 Calculating Day's Supply
6.2 IV Calculations
6.3 Measurement Conversions
6.4 Roman Numerals
6.5 Alligation

Source: Pharmacy Technician Certification Exam (PTCE) Blueprint

6.1 CALCULATING DAY'S SUPPLY

Day's supply is the amount of time the medication will last. Prescriptions do not always last 30 or 90 days and often require simple calculations in order to determine the day's supply. An incorrect day's supply can result in the patient receiving too much or too little of the medication, as well as insurance claim rejections on future refills. Day's supply can be determined by dividing the total number of doses to be dispensed by the number of doses taken day.

Capsules/Tablets

Example #1
Motrin (ibuprofen) 800mg, 1 tablet 3 times daily as needed, #30.

Days supply takes the maximum amount the patient could take in 1 day, in this case 3 tablets, divided into the amount dispensed of 30 pills.

30/3 = 10 days supply

Example #2
Toradol (ketorolac) 10mg, 1 tablet every 4-6 hours as needed, not more than 4 per day. #80.

Quantity of pills: 80 divided by 4 (maximum amount per day) = 20 days supply.

80/4 = 20 days supply

Example #3
Celexa (citalopram) 40mg, 1 tablet daily, #30.

30/1=30 days supply

These previous examples seem straightforward, but it gets a bit more complicated when you are dealing with other types of prescriptions.

Eye Drop

Calculating Ear Drop and Eye Drop Days Supply are different than the example problems above. Usually with ear and eye drops, 1ml (1 milliliter) will have 15 drops of medication. Time for another example.

Example #4

Tobramycin Eye Suspension, 1 drop into each eye 3 times daily, 5ml bottle.

1 drop into each eye=2 drops X 3 times daily = 6 drops per day

5ml X 15 drops per mL = 75 drops total

75 drops / 6 drops per day = 12.5 days supply

Topicals: Creams, Ointments, and Gels

These dosage forms require the pharmacy tech to calculate days supply using Fingertip Units. One fingertip unit = quantity of topical ointment/cream that when squeezed from a tube, reaches from the tip of an adult finger to the distal, or first crease of the index finger. One FTU is approximately 0.5g of the product.

Liquids: Solutions, Suspensions, Syrups

Example #5
Robutussin AC Syrup: Take 1 Teaspoonful Every 6 Hours As Needed for Cough, 4oz.

In this example, you need to be able to convert Ounces to Milliliters. There are 30 ML in 1 Oz.,

So 4 Oz = 120 ML. There are 5ML's in 1 Teaspoonful.

The maximum the patient could take in one day is 5ML times 4
(24 hours in 1 day, divided by 6 = 4) = 20ml used in one day.

120ML divided by 20ML = 6 Days Supply

Hopefully these examples have helped you to understand how to calculate days supply.

Chapter 6: *Pharmacy Math*

6.2 IV CALCULATIONS

It's easy to forget about the parenteral medications. Oral medications seem to be at the forefront of our minds while the other dosage forms are easily forgotten about. As a pharmacy technician, you will need to be able to perform the math necessary for accurate dosing of IV medications.

Some IV bags are hung with merely gravity helping them get the medication to the patient. Other IV medications are infused with the help of an infusion pump. These infusion pumps can be set to deliver IV medication at a factor known as the drop factor (gtt/mL).

This sounds similar to the flow rate (gtt/min). These 2 numbers can be found using the following equation:

$$\frac{\text{Volume (mL)}}{\text{Time (min)}} \times \text{Drop Factor (gtt/mL)} = \text{Flow Rate (gtt/min)}$$

Example: Calculate the flow rate for 600 mL of NS to be infused over 4 hours. The infusion set used is calibrated to a drop factor of 14 gtt/mL

$$\frac{600 \text{ mL}}{240 \text{ minutes}} \times 14 \text{ gtt/mL} = \boxed{35 \text{ gtt/min}}$$

Additionally you may be asked to figure out the Flow Rate, Time for Infusion, or Volume Infused of an IV administered medication. To solve this problem you will need to use the equation

(Rate)(Time) = Volume

Example:
How long will it take to infuse 500 mL of NS if it is infused at a rate of 75 mL an hour:

(75 mL/60 min)(Time) = 500 mL
Time = 400 min

6.3 MEASUREMENT CONVERSIONS

Pharmacy Techs must know the core measurement conversions in order to decode prescription orders, accurately translate instructions, and correctly mix solutions. The list of conversions on this page are the basics, and should suffice for the purpose of studying for the PTCB exam.. Please understand that some of the measurements are rounded up, in order to simplify memorization.

Dry	Liquid
1 OZ = 30 Gram 1 Lb = 454 Grams 1 Kg = 2.2 Lb 1 Gram = 15 Grain 1 Grain = 65 mg	1mL = 1CC 5mL = 1 Tsp 15mL = 1 Tbsp 30mL = 1 Ounce 480mL = 1 Pint 3840mL = 1 Gallon
Avoirdupois	**Metric**
3 Tsp = 1 Tbsp 2 Tbsp = 1 Oz 16 Oz = 1 Pint 2 Pint = 1 Qt 4 Qt = 1 Gallon 16 Oz = 1 Lb	1L = 1000mL 1Kg = 1000 Gram 1 Gram = 1000 mg 1 mg = 1000 mcg CC = Cm3

6.4 ROMAN NUMERALS

Roman numerals date back to ancient times when symbols were used for pharmaceutical computations and record keeping. Some physicians still use them in dosage calculations; therefore, pharmacy technicians must understand Roman numerals.

Common Roman Numerals used in pharmacies

I	1 - One
V	5 - Five
X	10 - Ten
L	50 - Fifty
SS	1/2 - Half

Chapter 6: *Pharmacy Math*

6.5 ALLIGATION

Alligation math is a short-cut often used by pharmacy technicians. Most pharmacy tech students initially refer to alligation as Tic-Tac-toe math, because a simple four line grid is used to organize the factors, which looks just like the popular children's strategy game of the same name.

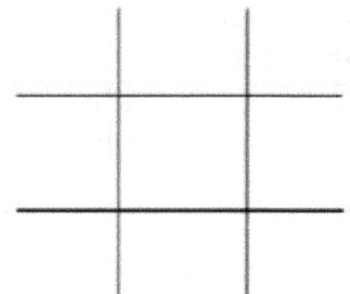

Sample Alligation Question

An order has arrived for <u>250mL of 2% solution.</u> You stock solutions of: 1 Gal. of 3% solution and 1 Gal. of 1% solution. You must mix together the two solutions to compound the custom ordered volume. How much of the 3% will you use?

Based on the question

→ You need 250mL a 2% solution
→ You have 1% and 3% solutions

How To Use Alligation Math

    Steps 1 First, Draw a tic-tac-toe grid

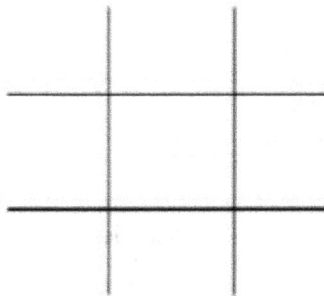

    Step 2

        Higher % strength top left →
        Desired % Strength in middle →
        Lower % strength bottom left →

Step 3

Calculate the difference between the bottom left number and the middle number going up diagonally. (Not adding or subtracting them, just finding the difference.)

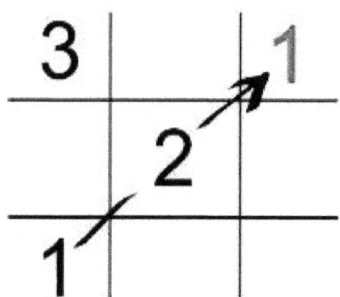

Step 4

Do the same thing from the top left, down. Again figuring the difference between the numbers.

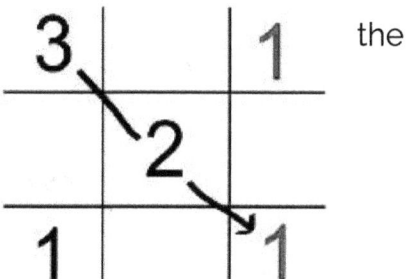

Step 5 Add the parts

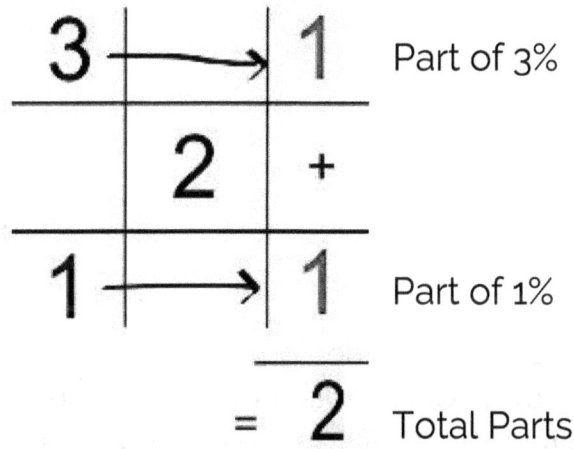

Part of 3%

Part of 1%

= 2 Total Parts

Step 6 Now, take a look back at the question and look for the total volume needed.

250 ML / 2 parts = 125 ML

The Answer

The question asked how much 3% to use. So, that's :1 part **X 125mL = 125mL of the 3%**

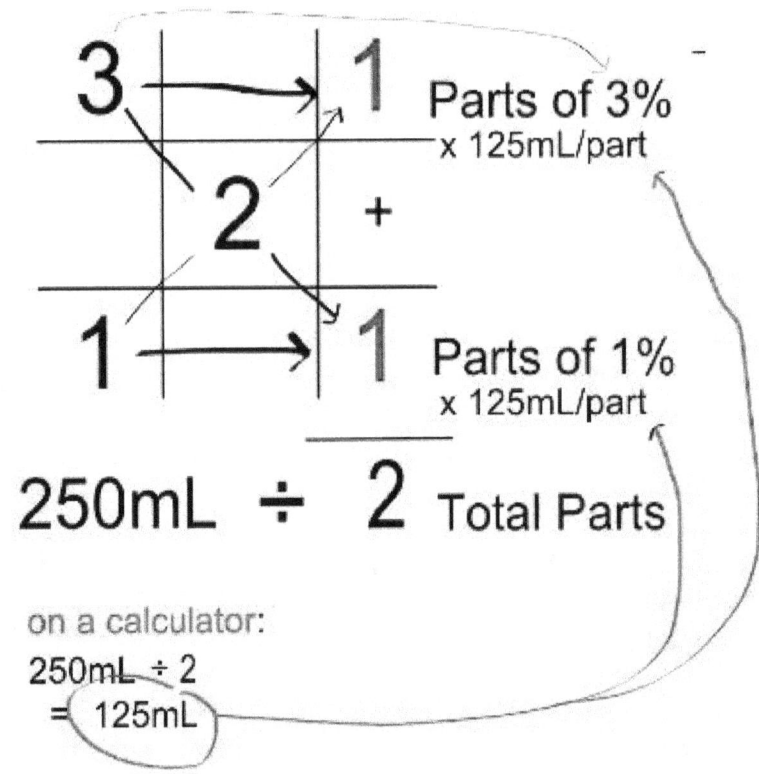

6.6 MEDICAL DOSAGE CALCULATIONS

Young's Rule

Pediatric formula based on Age. This one is valid for a patients under the age of 12. In children who are within average body weight for their, Young's and Clark's rule formulas are usually very close. When you're taking the PTCB or even just a practice quiz, if you're given only an age and asked to calculate a pediatric dosage, default to Young's rule.

$$\text{Adult Dose} \times \left(\frac{\text{Age}}{\text{Age} + 12} \right) = \text{Childs Dose}$$

Example: 11 year old girl / 70 Lbs

$$500mg \times (11 \div (11+12)) = \text{Child's Dose}$$

$$500mg \times (11 \div 23) = \text{Child's Dose}$$

$$500mg \times .48 = \text{Child's Dose}$$

Child's Dose = 240mg

Body Surface Area

This formula is Based on Height and weight (in Lbs.), and used in applications that require pinpoint accuracy. It's commonly used to dose cancer patients to achieve optimal treatment and prevent chemotherapy under-dosing / over-dosing.

$$BSA(m2) = \sqrt{(\text{inches} \times \text{lbs}) \div 3131}$$

Example: 132 Lb woman is prescribed Acyclovir 5mg/kg

First convert Lbs. to Kg

$$(132 \div 2.2) = 60kg$$

The prescription calls for 5mg per kg

$$60 \times 5mg = \textbf{300mg}$$

Chapter 6: *Pharmacy Math*

Chapter 7
Medication Order Entry and Fill Process

Rx Health Academy

General Information

As a pharmacy technician, it will be vital that you follow the many regulations and procedures to ensure the delivery of a quality product and to safeguard customer health and safety. This study guide outlines what you need to know in order to answer questions of this nature correctly on the PTCB exam. Approximately 17% of the questions require knowledge of this area of pharmacy tech work.

What you'll learn in this chapter

- Order entry process
- Intake, interpretation, and data entry
- Calculate doses required
- Fill process
- Labeling requirements
- Packaging requirements
- Dispensing process

Chapter Outline

7.1 Order Entry Process
7.2 Fill Process
7.3 Labeling
7.4 Packaging and Dispensing Process

Chapter 7: *Medication Order Entry and Fill Process*

7.1 ORDER ENTRY

To correctly fill a prescription, there are certain processes that must be followed in *order entry*. These processes include obtaining patient information, translating the prescription (which may include calculations), entering the order into the computer system, filling the prescription, and verifying the prescription and patient counseling.

Patient Information

It is very important to obtain all necessary patient information during your first encounter. Not doing so can delay a prescription. *Patient information* should include the full name of the patient, address, date of birth, telephone number, allergies to medications, insurance information, medical conditions, whether patient is waiting for prescription or not, and HIPAA compliance approval.

Translating the Prescription

A prescription has the following parts: patient information (such as name and address), prescriber information (including DEA number for controlled substances), date, name of drug, quantity to dispense, directions for use, number of refills, prescriber signature, *dispense as written* (DAW) or generic allowed (see chapter 8), and security markings for authentication of the prescription.

```
            FOUR SEASONS MEDICAL GROUP
                 Professional Building
             100 East South Street, Suite 200
        Figure 7.1 nton, PA 18515
                    PH: (111) 333-2211
_____
1
 Name  Joe Fleming          Date  Sept. 4, 2008
 Address  North Street, Scranton, PA 18512
2
 R
       3  Prozac Capsules 20 mg

       4  Dispense #30

       5  Sig.: one capsule each morning

                      6  Jonas Jones, M.D.
            7       Signature _____
    Repeat #   1    Printed Signature  Jonas Jones, M.D.
```

Parts of a prescription:

1. The name and address of the patient, and the date
2. The symbol Rx
3. The name of the medicine, its dose form, and the strength of the medicine
4. Directions to the pharmacist
5. Directions to the patient
6. The prescriber's signature
7. Refill information

Entering the Order in the Computer System

Each prescription entered into the computer system will be assigned a unique prescription number called the "Rx number" When a prescription is refilled, it will keep that same prescription number. Should a prescription be out of refills, the doctor will need to be contacted for approval. Controlled substance prescriptions <u>cannot</u> be refilled early due to the potential for abuse of the drug.

Here are the different types of ways prescriptions are sent to the pharmacy:

Type	Note
Written prescription	A written prescription for drugs MUST be legibly printed or typed and contain all of the elements of a prescription label.
Faxed prescription	Faxed prescriptions should include the physician's office letterhead and the manual signature of the practitioner. *Some states may require a statement of validity to be sent with the prescription orders
Called-in prescription	The prescription is called in by an prescribing individual and transcribes by the pharmacist on a pharmacy approved prescription pad. *Some states allow pharmacy interns to take phone orders
E-scripts prescription	Electronic prescribing or e-prescribing (e-Rx) is the computer-based electronic generation, transmission and filling of a medical prescription, taking the place of paper and faxed prescription
CPOE prescription	Computerized physician order entry (CPOE) is the process of a medical professional entering medication orders or other physician instructions electronically instead of on paper charts.

Chapter 7: *Medication Order Entry and Fill Process*

Filling the Prescription

The technician will first take the computer-generated label and find the correct drug. The drug should be verified by matching the 10-digit National Drug Code (NDC) number. Then the correct quantity should be counted out or poured into an appropriate size bottle. Prescriptions will be dispensed with a child-resistant cap unless indicated otherwise by the patient.

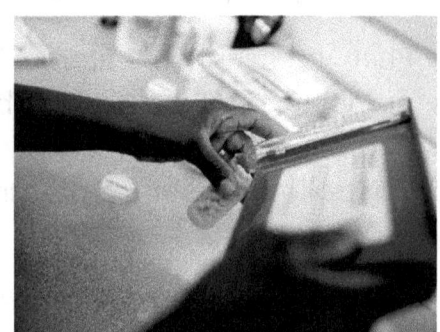

Figure 7.2.a

Here are the parts of the label a Pharmacy Technician affixes to the patient's medication packaging:

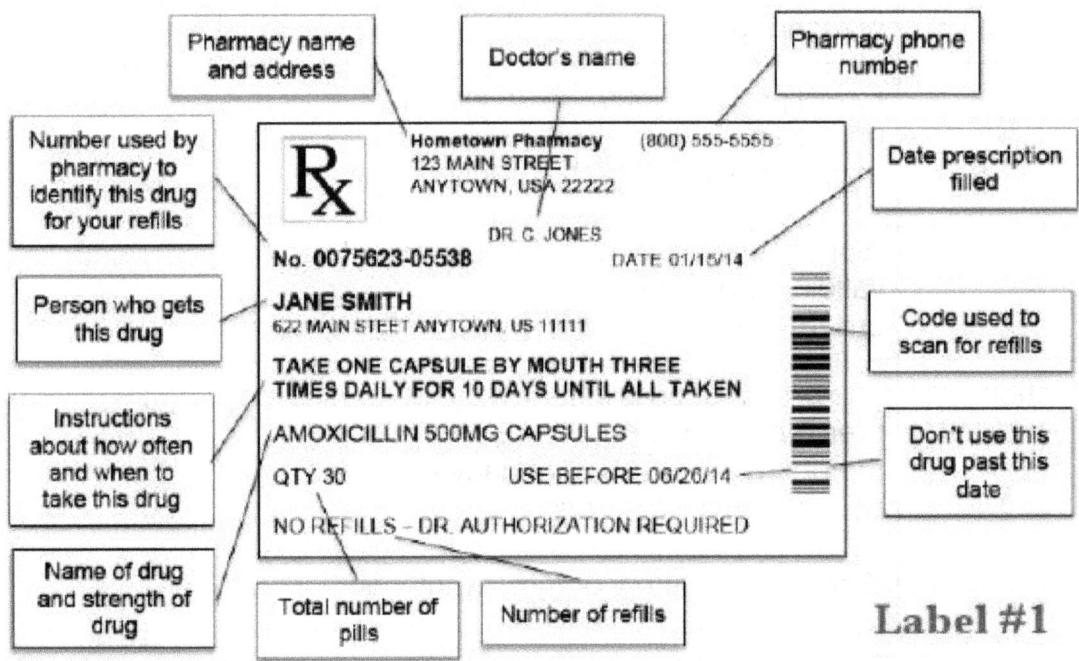

Label #1

Verification and Patient Consultation

The technician should leave the prescription and any original stock bottles for pharmacist verification. When the patient returns to pick up the prescription, the technician should verify the correct prescription for the patient by asking for a telephone number, date of birth, or address. Patients should also be asked if they have any questions for the pharmacist.

Intake, Interpretation, and Data Entry

When the patient drops off the prescription, the technician needs to obtain all the necessary patient information mentioned in the patient information section. Next, the prescription sig (or directions), which contains abbreviations, needs to be translated. Calculations may be necessary before entering the prescription into the computer system.

Calculation of Required Doses

One of the most common calculations a technician will need to do is to calculate the correct days supply of a medication so a patient receives the correct quantity. Days supply is calculated by dividing the total number of doses by the number of doses taken per day. For example, dispensing 30 tablets that are taken 3 times daily provides a 10-day supply (30÷3=10). You may also need to convert between units such as milliliters and fluid ounces, milliliters and units (for insulin), and grams and "doses" (for creams and ointments). Be sure you are fluent in this type of calculation.

7.2 FILL PROCESS

The fill process begins after the label is printed. It involves selecting the right product, handling the medication correctly, measuring out the correct quantity, and doing final preparations.

Selecting the Right Product

Figure 7.2.a

When filling a prescription, selecting the right drug is one of the most important steps in the filling process. The technician should check to make sure the correct drug has been chosen by first comparing the drug name on the bottle/container to the prescription label. Then the technician should check the NDC number on the drug bottle with the one printed on the label.

Dealing with Handling Requirements

Some drugs may have special handling requirements. For example, prescription labels for oral inhalers will need to be attached to the inhaler itself. Nitroglycerin should be dispensed in the original bottle. The small nitroglycerin bottle cannot have a label attached so it will be necessary to place it in a pharmacy bottle and attach the label to the pharmacy bottle.

Measurement

Solid dosage forms of medication, like tablets or capsules, may be counted by hand, dispensed by dispensing machines or be pre-packaged in blister packs to help with patient adherence. Liquids, creams and other dosage forms may need to be poured out or transferred to the appropriate sized container when being filled.

Final Preparations

The prescription, stock bottle (if available) and filled medication should be left for the final pharmacist check. In some states and settings, such as hospitals or long-term care pharmacies, technicians may be allowed to check other technician's work. Often these technicians that can check will be required to obtain additional training.

7.3 LABELING

Prescriptions may have special labeling needs. This special labeling, using auxiliary and warning labels, is a way to communicate important information to the patient.

Auxiliary and Warning Labels

Auxiliary and *warning labels* provide extra, important information for the patient that is not found in the prescription's directions. These labels may give warnings about potential side effects like "may cause drowsiness" or the labels may let the patient know the medication should be taken with food or that it needs to be refrigerated.

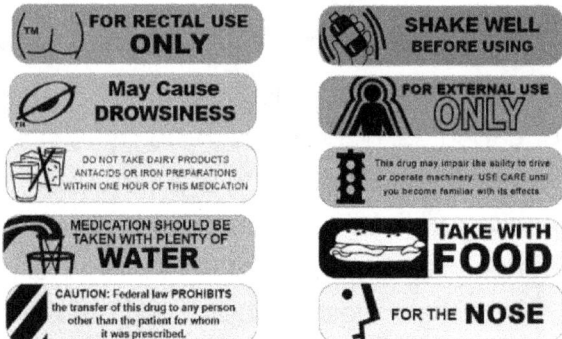

Figure 7.3.a

Expiration Date

Some medications may only be stable for a certain amount of time. In this case, the prescription will need to be labeled with an expiration date. For example, reconstituted antibiotics may only be stable for 10 days. In a hospital setting, IV solutions may need to be used in a couple of hours or less.

If a stock bottle of medication has an expiration date listed as 08/2020 this means the medication is no longer good to use on 08/01./2020.

7.4 PACKAGING AND DISPENSING PROCESS

During the packaging process, some drugs require patient-specific information, as well as informational sheets. Packaging includes the following specific requirements that are mentioned below. The dispensing process may vary from facility to facility, however, you will need to understand the basics of dispensing medication to patients.

Patient-Specific Information

Some drugs require that patient informational pamphlets be dispensed with a patient's prescription. Some drugs are required to be dispensed with *black box warning* informational sheets. These sheets tell a patient how to safely take a drug and what to look out for. Most pharmacies also provide informational sheets that list common side effects of the drug.

Packaging Requirements

Drugs can be dispensed in a variety of vehicles. Examples of these are IV bags, syringes, and plastic and glass bottles. Technicians may be required to perform calculations, such as IV calculations, in order to dispense the drug correctly. All prescriptions are dispensed with a child-resistant cap unless the patient requests otherwise. Many pharmacies will also dispense the drugs in light-resistant bottles due to the fact that some drugs are not stable when exposed to light.

The Dispensing Process

Figure 7.4.a

When a patient comes to pick up a prescription, the technician will retrieve the prescription from the storage area. The technician should then ask for the patient's personal information (name, date of birth, address, and telephone number) for verification.

The patient should be asked if he or she has any questions for the pharmacists. Many states and pharmacies require patients to then sign a log to show they picked up the prescription and/or that counseling was offered and refused. The patient may need to pay a copay before leaving. Be aware that, as a pharmacy technician, you may also be required to calculate the amount of this copay, according to the patient's insurance policy.

Chapter 7: *Medication Order Entry and Fill Process*

Worksheet 7a: Medication Order Entry and Fill Process

1. List the seven steps of the order entry process.

    1. _____
    2. _____
    3. _____
    4. _____
    5. _____
    6. _____
    7. _____

2. <u>Patient information</u> should include: the full name of the patient, address, date of birth, telephone number, _____, insurance information, medical conditions, whether patient is waiting for prescription or not, and _____.

3. Non-controlled and controlled substance prescriptions can be refilled early. True or false?

    True   **False**

4. List the three ways solid dosage forms like tablets or capsules may be measured during the fill process.

    _____   _____   _____

5. Provide two examples (not given in the text) for common auxiliary labels used during the labeling of pharmaceutical products below.

    _____   _____

6. During the dispensing process, the technician should then ask for the patient's personal information for verification. Which of the following is the correct information for verification?

    a) Name, date of birth, and member ID #
    b) Name, address, and telephone number
    c) Name, date of birth, address, and telephone number
    d) Name, member ID #, and telephone number

Chapter 7: *Medication Order Entry and Fill Process*

Medication Order Entry And Fill Process Quiz

1. _____ requires community pharmacists to offer counseling to Medicaid patients regarding medications.
    a) OBRA
    b) The FDA
    c) The DEA
    d) HIPAA

2. An NDC number is _____ digits long and is _____ for all drugs.
    a) 8; different
    b) 8; the same
    c) 10; different
    d) 10; the same

3. Patient information that must be entered into the computer includes the patient's _____
    a) Name and date of birth
    b) Telephone number and address
    c) Medication allergies and medication safety cap preference
    d) All of the above

4. A signature log is used in a pharmacy
    a) To log medications that need to be ordered
    b) For patients to sign for prescription received
    c) To document patient signatures for their patient profile
    d) By pharmacists to document prescriptions filled

5. A PRN order is an order for a medication that is used on a(n)
    a) Twice a day
    b) Daily
    c) As needed
    d) Immediate

6. In the NDC number 0415-5258-26, the last two numbers indicate the
    a) Dosage form
    b) Manufacturer
    c) Package size
    d) Drug strength

7. How many tablets should be dispensed, given the following order?
   Amoxicillin 250 mg tabs; sig 1 tab BID X 10 days
   a) 10
   b) 20
   c) 30
   d) 40

8. A drug container has the expiration date of 07/2018. On which of the following days does this bottle actually expire?
   a) 6/30/2018
   b) 7/01/2018
   c) 7/31/2018
   d) 8/01/2018

9. Which of the following pieces of information is NOT located on the prescription label?
   a) Pharmacy name
   b) Prescriber's name
   c) Medication strength
   d) Prescriber's address

10. Which of the following is NOT a valid method for presenting a prescription for a noncontrolled medication?
    a) Via mail to retail pharmacy
    b) Submitted to a pharmacy as an e-script
    c) Presented to a pharmacy in person
    d) Faxed to a pharmacy

Chapter 7: *Medication Order Entry and Fill Process*

Quiz: Study Guide

Question Number	Section Reference
1	2.3
2	2.2
3	7.1
4	2.2
5	7.1
6	2.2
7	4.5, 6.2
8	7.3
9	7.1
10	7.1

Chapter References

Figure 7.1.a: http://www.op.nysed.gov/images/pharmacy_sm.jpg;
Figure 7.1.b: http://d279m997dpfwgl.cloudfront.net/wp/2016/09/0914_drugs-1000x667.jpg

Figure 7.2.a:
https://article.images.consumerreports.org/prod/content/dam/CRO%20Images%202018/Health/November/CR-Health-InlineHero-COuld-Your-Drugstore-Be-Your-Doctor-11-18

Figure 7.3.a: https://pharmlabs.unc.edu/labs/images/labels.gif

Figure 7.4.a:
https://s3-us-west-2.amazonaws.com/jobcorps.gov/styles/fs_bg_img_sm/s3/2017-10/JC_Career_Pharmacy-Technician-2_0.jpg?h=d1fbde62&itok=SV3Pe6Bp; Figure 7.4.b:

Chapter 8
Pharmacy Inventory Management

Rx Health Academy

General Information

Maintaining the organization and care of pharmaceuticals will be part of your role as a pharmacy technician. This study guide lists some of the most important guidelines for inventory management.

What you'll learn in this chapter

- Function and application of NDC, lot numbers and expiration dates
- Formulary or approved/preferred product list
- Ordering and receiving processes
- Storage requirements
- Removal

Chapter Outline

8.1 Using Numerical Information
8.2 Product Lists
8.3 Ordering and Receiving

Chapter 8: Pharmacy Inventory Management

8.1 USING NUMERICAL INFORMATION

Numerical information of a drug gives important information, such as where and when the drug was manufactured and the expiration date of the drug. This information can be found in the National Drug Code (NDC) numbers, lot numbers, and expiration dates.

National Drug Code (NDC) Numbers

The National Drug Code (NDC) is a three-segment, 10-digit number that identifies the labeler or manufacturer, product, and package size of the drug. The first segment identifies the manufacturer or labeler of the drug. The second segment identifies the drug strength, dosage form, and formulation. The third segment identifies the drug form and size.

Lot Numbers

A drug stock bottle will also contain a *lot number* on it's packaging that is a unique number given to each batch of drugs during the manufacturing process. Should a drug manufacturer need to recall a drug, it will usually be done by lot number. This way, a pharmacy can pull the affected lot numbers, but keep the drug stock that is not affected by a recall.

Expiration Dates

A drug manufacturer will also place an expiration date on each drug packaging. This includes both prescription and over-the-counter drugs. Sometimes, pharmacies may repackage the drugs. In this case, the expiration date will be set as 1 year from the date of repackaging or the manufacturer's expiration date, whichever comes first. Technicians will be required to check for expiration dates. Sometimes this date is called the beyond use date.

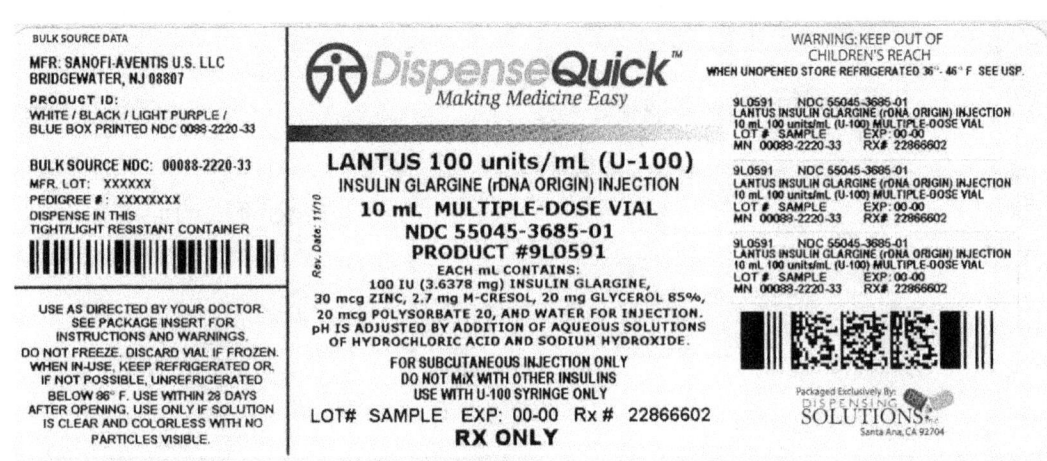

Figure 8.1.a

8.2 PRODUCT LISTS

Product lists (or formularies) are approved lists of drugs a hospital pharmacy will utilize to fill prescriptions or hospital orders. This list is developed by the hospital's *Pharmacy and Therapeutics (P&T) Committee*.

Generic

As mentioned in chapter 1, a *generic drug* is a drug that is manufactured by a different manufacturer than the original developer of a drug. For a generic drug to be considered bioequivalent, or the same chemically, it must be equal to the brand name drug in the following ways: active ingredient, route of administration, dosage form, use, and the performance of the drug.

Therapeutic Substitution

A *therapeutic substitution* is the substitution of a drug with a drug that is chemically different but exerts the same clinical effect. Some reasons a therapeutic substitution may be made include the prescribed drug is not on the formulary, a drug is out of stock, and the prescribed drug is too expensive or it is not covered by the insurance. The prescriber, in most cases, will need to be contacted by the pharmacy for a therapeutic substitution to be made.

Figure 8.2.a

Dispense as Written

When a prescriber indicates a prescription should be filled as *dispense as written*, this means it should be filled with the brand name medication and a generic cannot be used. Reasons for this include the patient has allergy issues, the patient responds better to the brand name drug, or the patient prefers the brand name drug.

8.3 ORDERING AND RECEIVING

Pharmacy technicians have a role in maintaining adequate stock levels in the pharmacy. This is accomplished by maintaining stock levels and rotating stock.

Chapter 8: *Pharmacy Inventory Management*

Maintaining Par Levels

Par level is the minimum amount of stock of a drug that should be kept on hand. When stock falls below this level, it is time to reorder a drug. Many pharmacies will utilize a *periodic automatic replenishment (PAR) system* for the reordering of drugs. This system will automatically track drug stock levels. However, the pharmacy staff is able to adjust the order as needed.

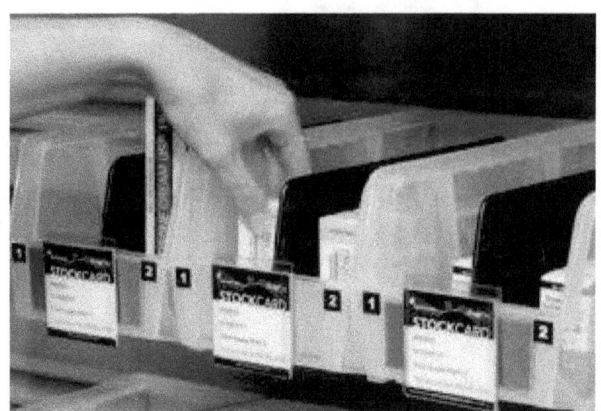

Figure 8.3.a

Stock Rotation

Drugs should be rotated so that the drug with the earliest expiration date is on the shelf first. This way, the oldest drug stock will be used first and has less of a chance of expiring before it is used. This also makes it easier for the pharmacy staff to check expiration dates and remove expired drug product as needed. Most pharmacies remove medications from stock two months prior to expiration.

Documentation

Pharmacies may be required to keep logs of certain areas of pharmacy operations including: refrigerator and freezer temperature readings, air temperatures, when equipment was serviced and cleaned, air quality testing results, and calibration of pharmacy equipment.

Storage

All drugs used in the pharmacy have storage requirements. Drugs can be kept at room temperature, under refrigeration, or in the freezer depending upon drug storage requirements. Room temperature is defined as between 68 and 77 degrees Fahrenheit (F). Refrigerated drugs need to be kept at 36 to 46 degrees F. Drugs stored in the freezer are kept between −13 to 14 degrees F. If a drug has no specific storage requirements, it should be kept at room temperature.

Removal

At times, it may be necessary to remove a medication from stock. This can be due to drug recalls or drug returns of expired drug product.

Recalls

Drug recalls can be initiated by either the drug manufacturer or FDA. There are three classes of drug recalls. These classes are:

Class	Description
Class I	is the most severe type of recall and involves medication that is likely to cause severe adverse effects or even death. This can also occur if one drug is labeled as another drug.
Class II	occurs when medication may cause temporary adverse health effects that are reversible or if there is a small risk of serious adverse effects.
Class III	is the least severe type of recall. The medication in question is not likely to cause a patient to have adverse effects.

Returns

If a patient returns a prescription drug, that drug cannot be returned to stock. It must be kept in a quarantine spot in the pharmacy for disposal or return to the drug manufacturer.

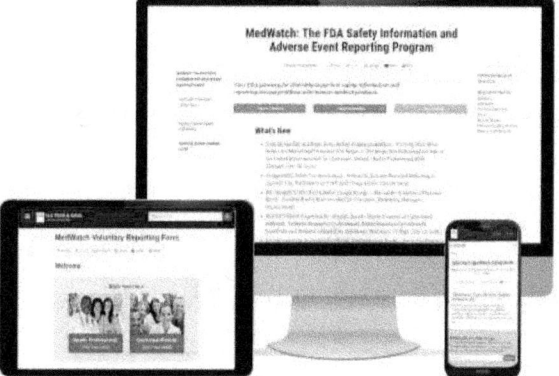

Figure 8.3.b

Updates

Once a drug is approved, drug safety is still monitored by the FDA. One way the FDA accomplishes this is by its *MedWatch program*. Through the MedWatch program, patients are able to report problems with a particular drug directly to the FDA. There is an online reporting system for the patients to utilize.

Reverse Distribution

Reverse distribution occurs when a pharmacy sends outdated, unusable drug product back to the drug manufacturer or other authorized distributor for processing or disposal. This may occur when drugs are returned by patients or the drugs are expired.

Chapter 8: *Pharmacy Inventory Management*

Worksheet 8a: Pharmacy Inventory Management

1. Identify the numerical information on the sample prescription label provided below.

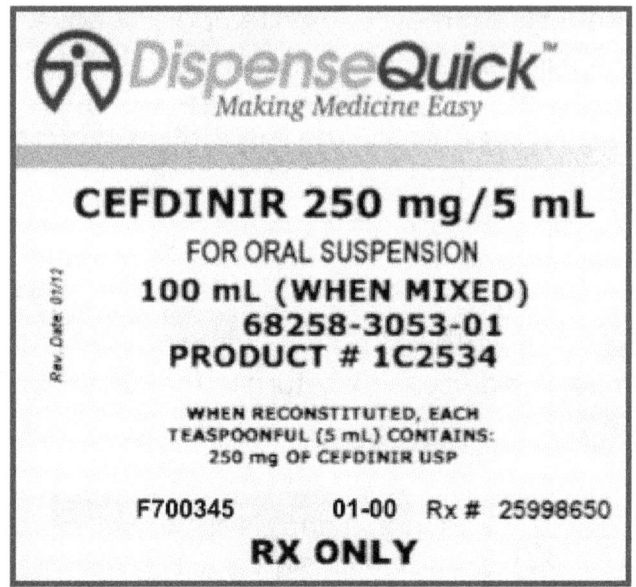

2. Formularies are developed by a hospital's Pharmacy and Therapeutics (P&T) Committee and are used to fill prescriptions or hospital orders. True or false?

   True   **False**

3. According to the text, for a generic drug to be considered bioequivalent to a brand name drug, it must be equal to the brand name in the following ways: _____, _____, dosage form, use, and the _____ of the drug.

4. List the three (3) characteristics of both terms below:

Generic Drug	**Therapeutic Substitution**

Worksheet 8b: Pharmacy Inventory Management

5. What is the title of the PAR system?
   a) Pharmaceutical automatic restock system
   b) Periodic automatic replenishment system
   c) Pharmaceutical automated replenishment system
   d) Periodic automated restock system

6. Drug recalls can only initiated by the FDA. True or false?

   True   **False**

7. Under what two circumstances does <u>reverse distribution</u> occur?

   _____   _____

8. Give an example of a <u>Class I Recall</u>.

   _____

Pharmacy Inventory Management Quiz

1. Which of the following is an example of a Class I recall?
   a) A drug recall is issued when there is a strong likelihood that the product will cause serious adverse effects or death
   b) A drug recall is issued when there is a likelihood of temporary or reversible adverse effects
   c) A drug recall is issued when exposure to the product is unlikely to cause adverse drug effects
   d) None of the above

2. The National Drug Code (NDC) contains 10 numbers. The first set of numbers indicates the _____.
   a) Labeler
   b) Product
   c) Quantity
   d) Interactions

3. Who may be responsible for initiating the drug recall process?
   a) FDA
   b) DEA
   c) CDC
   d) Pharmacy

4. True or False: Pharmacy technicians do not participate in medication inventory procedures.

5. What is a PAR?
   a) A system to determine recalls
   b) A robot to help fill prescriptions
   c) An automatic system used to help control inventory
   d) A computer program that examines potential side effects

6. MedWatch is a monitoring system used by the FDA for consumers to report _____.
   a) Adverse drug reactions
   b) Concerns with pricing
   c) Requests for medication coupons
   d) Discrepancies with pharmacy personnel

Chapter 8: *Pharmacy Inventory Management*

7. A beyond use date is used to indicate the
    a) Product expiration
    b) Recall status
    c) Lot number
    d) NDC number

8. True or False: NDC numbers are the same for each medication within a drug class.

9. Who develops and maintains a hospital's formulary?
    a) Hospital business office
    b) Pharmacy department
    c) Insurance companies
    d) Pharmacy and Therapeutics (P&T) Committee

10. Pharmacy refrigerators should be maintained at a temperature of
    a) 36 °C to 46 °C
    b) 45 °C to 55 °C
    c) 2 °C to 8 °C
    d) 10 °C to 18 °C

Chapter 8: *Pharmacy Inventory Management*

Quiz: Study Guide

Question Number	Section Reference
1	8.2 , 2.4
2	2.2, 8.1
3	2.2
4	8.1
5	8.3
6	8.3
7	8.1
8	8.2 , 2.4
9	8.2
10	8.3

Chapter References

Figure 8.1.a: https://ndclist.com/assets/spl/images/f2149727-c2df-41b0-97f1-45ea75e0aa1a/NDC%2055045-3685-01------SANOFI-AVENTIS.jpg

Figure 8.2.a: http://gabi-journal.net/wp-content/uploads/Substitution-V13F14.jpg

Figure 8.3.a: https://www.mobileaspects.com/wp-content/uploads/2018/08/stock-card-300x199.jpg;
Figure 8.3.b: https://www.fda.gov/files/styles/large/public/medwatch_2019_1.jpg?itok=d4iourC7

Chapter 9
Pharmacy Billing and Reimbursment

Rx Health Academy

General Information

Billing insurance and planning reimbursements is a vital part of a pharmacy tech's job. Even though only about 8% of the questions on the PTCB Exam are devoted specifically to this topic, you'll need to be familiar with the concepts discussed in this study guide. Be sure to seek additional assistance in the comment section, especially in areas in which you have questions, as you prepare for the test.

What you'll learn in this chapter

- Reimbursement policies and plans
- Third party resolution
- Third-party reimbursement systems
- Healthcare reimbursement systems
- Coordination of benefits

Chapter Outline

9.1 Obtaining Patient Insurance Information
9.2 Key Terms
9.3 Types of Insurance Coverage
9.4 Managed Care Programs

9.1 OBTAINING PATIENT INSURANCE INFORMATION

Though providing quality medicinal therapy is the first concern of a pharmacy, obtaining payment for drugs and medical supplies dispensed to a patient is a duty of most pharmacy technicians. Handling payments and insurance claims might not seem as important as dispensing medications, but to the pharmacy, obtaining timely payment is critical to profitability.

After a medical claim is submitted, the insurance company determines their financial responsibility for the payment to the provider. This process is referred to as claims ***adjudication***.

The insurance company can decide to pay the claim in full, deny the claim, or to reduce the amount paid to the provider.As with all other aspects of pharmacy work, obtaining and storing current, accurate insurance information is vital to a well-managed pharmacy.

Understanding the work related to obtaining payment as well as being familiar with the various entities that provide payment is imperative for a valuable pharmacy technician. It's usually the duty of the Pharmacy Technician to obtain information regarding the method of payment for each prescription. Whether the patient is new to the pharmacy or a regular customer, it's good practice to ask for certain information each and every time a drug is dispensed.

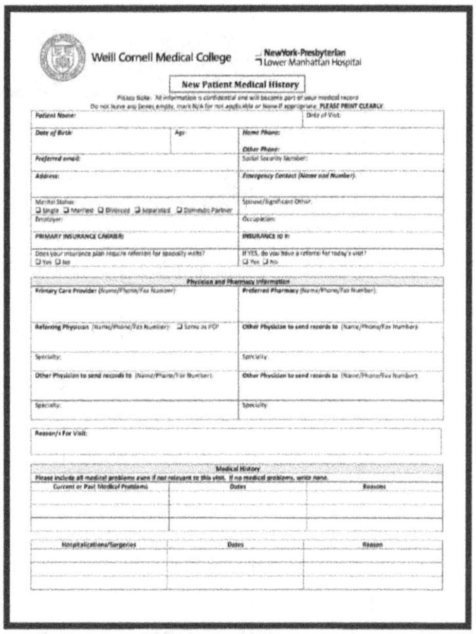
Weill Cornell Medical College
NewYork-Presbyterian Lower Manhattan Hospital
New Patient Medical History
PLEASE PRINT CLEARLY
Patient Name: | Date of Visit:
Date of Birth: | Age: | Home Phone: | Other Phone:
Preferred email: | Social Security Number:
Address: | Emergency Contact (Name and Number):
Marital Status: ☐ Single ☐ Married ☐ Divorced ☐ Separated ☐ Domestic Partner | Spouse/Significant Other:
Employer: | Occupation:
PRIMARY INSURANCE CARRIER: | INSURANCE ID #:
Does your insurance plan require referrals for specialty visits? ☐ Yes ☐ No | If YES, do you have a referral for today's visit? ☐ Yes ☐ No
Physician and Pharmacy Information
Primary Care Provider (Name/Phone/Fax Number): | Preferred Pharmacy (Name/Phone/Fax Number):
Referring Physician (Name/Phone/Fax Number): ☐ Same as PCP | Other Physician to send records to (Name/Phone/Fax Number):
Specialty: | Specialty:
Other Physician to send records to (Name/Phone/Fax Number): | Other Physician to send records to (Name/Phone/Fax Number):
Specialty: | Specialty:
Reason/s For Visit:
Medical History
Please include all medical problems even if not relevant to this visit. If no medical problems, write none.
Current or Past Medical Problems | Dates | Reasons
Hospitalizations/Surgeries | Dates | Reason

Figure 9.1.a

Employment and insurance plans change constantly, so it's standard practice to ask if there have been any changes since the last visit. Also, there are instances where the medication or supplies requested are related to a workers' compensation claim and shouldn't be billed to the patient's primary insurance.

If the patient is new to the pharmacy, he or she will need to complete the pharmacy's standard medical profile questionnaire. If the intake form doesn't ask for payment information, ask what method of payment can be expected. If the patient has insurance, ask for the current prescription drug benefit card to copy for the pharmacy's records. Verify that the insurance card presented is from the primary insurance plan, and ask if there's any secondary insurance coverage.

Before we discuss the types of health insurance coverage and the methods of obtaining payment for prescriptions dispensed, let's take a moment to become familiar with some terms related to health insurance.

9.2 KEY TERMS

The following terms are used frequently when working with health insurance claims and might be encountered when working in a pharmacy setting.

Coordination of benefits (COB) allows plans that provide health and/or prescription coverage for a person with Medicare to determine their respective payment responsibilities (i.e., determine which insurance plan has the primary payment responsibility

closed formulary A system in which specific drugs in each therapeutic class are covered. In a closed formulary, drugs that aren't on the formulary are either not covered at all or may require prior authorization.

coinsurance Most policies have some type of coinsurance, which is a method of cost-sharing that requires a group member to pay a stated percentage of all remaining eligible medical expenses after the deductible has been paid. For example, a patient pays 20 percent of the cost of the drug and the insurance company picks up the remaining 80 percent. Cost per prescription will vary based on the cost of the drug.

co-payment, or copay A specified dollar amount that a member must pay out-of-pocket for a service or prescription. For example, a patient might have a copay of $5 for all generic prescriptions. That means that whether the drug costs $10 or $200, the patient pay $5 per fill. Techs are often required to obtain the copayment at the time the medication is dispensed.

deductible A flat amount an insured patient must pay before the insurer will make any benefit payments.

For example, a patient has a $250 deductible, which means that the patient pays full price for the first $250 of medications.

- Once that $250 is paid, the insurance benefit kicks in, and most patients will then pay either a percentage of the cost of the drug or a copay.
- Normally, patients have to meet the deductible each and every plan year, which is why many patients pay much more out-of-pocket for their prescriptions at the beginning of the year than at the end of the year.
- Also, pharmacies tend to get very busy at the end of the year because most patients try to get as many prescriptions filled as possible before they have to meet a new annual deductible.
    - **Tip:** This is the best time of the year to find a new job.

dependents The spouse or children covered under an employee's insurance policy.

disease management (DM) A program of preventive, diagnostic, and therapeutic measures intended to provide cost-effective, quality healthcare for a patient population suffering from or at risk for specific chronic illnesses or conditions.

drug utilization review (DUR) A program that evaluates the safe, effective, and appropriate use of prescribed drugs.

eligibility The confirmation that the patient has coverage under a specified insurance plan. Techs often need to verify eligibility as part of the workflow of filling a prescription. Verification of eligibility is done is several ways, depending on the insurance provider.

exclusive provider organization (EPO) A healthcare benefit arrangement similar to a PPO, but without out-of-network coverage.

fee schedule The fee set by a managed care program to be acceptable for a procedure or service, which the provider agrees to accept as payment in full.

formulary A listing of drugs that are considered preferred therapy by a managed care program. The drugs listed are predetermined to be the best medications for cost by the program.

For example, drugs A, B, C, D, and E are all in the same drug class.

- The insurance company puts drugs A and B on the formulary. If a prescriber writes a prescription for drugs C, D, or E, the drugs will either not be covered at all or will cost the patient more because they're not on the formulary.
- These are referred to as non-formulary drugs. In this case, the pharmacy will often contact the prescriber to get the prescription changed to either drug A or B, which would be referred to as formulary alternatives or preferred drugs.
- Many insurance companies provide members with a pocket sized list of drugs on their specific formulary. It's a good idea to advise patients to bring their prescription plan formulary with them to their doctor's appointments.

generic substitution Dispensing a drug that's the generic equivalent of a drug listed on a pharmacy benefit management (PBM) plan's formulary. In some states, this can be done without physician approval.

health information network (HIN) A computerized system that links healthcare entities to exchange patient, clinical, and financial information in an effort to provide quality healthcare and reduce costs.

health maintenance organization (HMO) A form of health insurance providing various medical care within a group of physicians. Medical professionals offer care through the HMO for a flat monthly rate with no deductibles. Patients can use only physicians within the HMO network.

mail-order pharmacy programs Programs that offer plan members the benefit of obtaining drugs delivered through the mail at a reduced cost. Most mail-order programs allow patients to obtain a three-month supply at a lower cost than they would pay at a retail pharmacy. Some insurance plans actually require patients to use mail order for maintenance medications and set a limit of how many times a patient can get these medications filled at a retail pharmacy.

managed care program A system that manages the cost and quality of healthcare for a group of individuals.

open formulary A system in which drugs on both a preferred list and not on the preferred list will be covered by a pharmacy benefit manager or managed care organization. For example, drug A is on the preferred list and drug B is on the non-preferred list. Both drugs are covered on the plan, but the patient will pay more for drug B since it's nonpreferred.

out-of-pocket costs What the member pays toward plan expenses that aren't reimbursed. Deductibles, premiums, and copays would all be considered out-of-pocket expenses.

override An override can be considered to be an exception to the rule. For example, a patient comes to the pharmacy to get a medication filled and the drug plan rejects the claim because the member is trying to get it filled too soon. The member tells you he or she is going on vacation and will run out while out of town. You call the insurance to get a vacation override to get the drug covered by the plan, because this circumstance is an exception to the rule that medications can't be filled early.

pharmaceutical cards Identification cards issued by a PBM to plan members. Also known as prescription cards or drug cards. pharmacy benefit manager (PBM) An organization set up to contain drug costs, while providing safe and more efficient use of prescription medications. The PBM is often different from the patient's actual medical insurance, which can be quite confusing for many patients and pharmacy staff members. The billing information for the PBM is usually contained on the patient's medical insurance card, but is often hard to find. Sometimes it's only identifiable by a symbol or a code that's often in small print. Sometimes, the prescription insurance information is on the back of the patient's medical insurance card. Occasionally, the prescription insurance information is on a separate card.

plan limitations Some insurance plans set specific limits as to how many of certain medications they'll pay for in a month's time based on FDA-approved dosing. Many times, drugs are prescribed for unapproved uses and require higher doses.

Also, since some patients respond differently to drugs, higher doses are needed to treat the patient appropriately.

For example, drug A is approved to be dosed at one pill per day, but a patient needs to take two pills a day. Since the drug plan has a quantity limit restrictions on this drug, the physician will need to contact the drug plan to get this medication covered for the patient.

policy limitations Some insurance policies exclude certain conditions from payment. Typical conditions that are often excluded from coverage are work-related injuries, pre-existing conditions, and nontraditional treatments.

preauthorization Prior approval from the insurance company that's necessary before certain testing, procedures, and treatments (including medications) can be obtained.

preferred provider organization (PPO) A healthcare system that provides medical services for a reduced cost by encouraging patients to use designated healthcare providers who contract with the PPO at a discount. However, a PPO does allow patients to seek care by healthcare providers who are outside the PPO network for an additional expense.

prior authorization In pharmacy, a procedure that requires a prescriber to obtain permission to prescribe a medication prior to prescribing it in order to reduce costs. Also called prior approval.

step therapy With step therapy, certain costly drugs are covered only if less-expensive, preferred alternatives have already been tried. For example: drug A and drug B are both used to treat stomach ulcers, but drug B is much more expensive than drug A. The plan will require the patient to try and fail on drug A before they'll pay for drug B. The prescriber must provide documentation to the insurance company that the patient has failed on drug A. Drug B is considered a step- up from drug A.

tiered copayment system In a plan that has a tiered copay system, drugs are separated into different categories (usually three) based on their cost and function. As the tier, or level, increases, so does the member's out-of-pocket expense. For example, many plans now have 3 tiers:

- *Tier 1* includes all generic drugs,
- *Tier 2* may be preferred name-brand drugs, and
- *Tier 3* may include all non-preferred name-brand drugs. A plan may require a member to pay $5 for drugs in tier 1, $15 for drugs in tier 2, and $50 for drugs in tier 3. Drug plans differ in what drugs are in each tier, and what the cost to the member will be for drugs in each specific tier.

9.3 TYPES OF INSURANCE COVERAGE

As you learned previously, a *third-party payer* is the party providing payment for services other than the patient. The most common third-party payers for prescriptions include:

- Government plans, such as Medicare, Medicaid, TRICARE, and CHAMPVA
- Managed-care programs, such as HMOs and PPOs
- Private insurance companies, such as Blue Cross Blue Shield and Aetna
- Pharmacy benefit managers (PBMs), such as Express Scripts and MedImpact
- Workers' compensation

To better understand how prescription payment plans work, let's take a closer look at each type of third-party payer.

Medicare

Both the Medicare and Medicaid programs were created under the Social Security Act in 1965. After several governmental changes, Medicare and Medicaid are now administered by the *Centers for Medicare & Medicaid Services (CMS)*.

Medicare is a national health insurance program for individuals age 65 and older, as well as individuals under the age of 65 with qualifying disabilities. In addition, Medicare also covers individuals with end-stage renal disease (ESRD).

Today, Medicare coverage is divided into four parts.

Chart 9.3.a

Medicare Part A	Provides coverage on inpatient hospital services, skilled-nursing facility services, home health services, and hospice care.
Medicare Part B	Provides payment for services rendered by physicians and outpatient hospital care, as well as certain services not covered under Medicare Part A. Medicare Part B also covers some home healthcare supplies, including diabetic testing machines and supplies, nebulizer machines and the drugs used in them (for certain conditions), as well as canes,

	crutches, wheelchairs, and various other types of *durable medical equipment* (DME).
Medicare Part C	Known as *Medicare Advantage*, this plan is available to patients entitled to Medicare Part A and enrolled in Medicare Part B. Qualifying patients who reside in the plan's service area are entitled to switch to Medicare Advantage. Patients enrolled in Medicare Advantage are typically limited to a network of specific physicians, specialists, and hospitals under the plan, except in an emergency. Under Medicare Advantage, patients are offered a number of managed-care options to choose from. Patients may pay lower copays and receive additional benefits not available under Parts A and B.
Medicare Part D	Drug coverage became available to qualifying individuals in 2006 under the *Medicare Prescription Drug Improvement and Modernization Act (MMA) of 2003.* Separate drug insurance can be obtained by purchasing optional Part D coverage. Persons previously covered under union or pension health plans aren't required to purchase Part D as long as their current plan is considered comparable to Part D or their previous plan dissolves. After meeting an annual deductible, Medicare Part D covers certain drug costs based on the amount spent on drugs per year. Limited-income seniors and persons with qualifying disabilities might receive additional financial aid from the Social Security Administration (SSA) toward prescription payments and plan premiums.

Medicaid

The Medicaid program provides medical and health-related services to qualified persons with needs. Medicaid is administered by each state under federal guidelines and with federal funding. To receive matching federal funding, states must adhere to guidelines for basic services. If states choose to include additional services, such as prescription drug coverage, they receive additional federal funding. If a patient has both Medicare and Medicaid coverage, Medicare is considered the primary coverage and must be billed first.

TRICARE and CHAMPVA

TRICARE is the healthcare program for dependents of military personnel in the United States. TRICARE was formerly known as CHAMPUS. *CHAMPVA* provides medical coverage for families of veterans with total, permanent, service-connected disabilities, as well as coverage for surviving spouses and dependents of veterans who died in the line of duty.

9.4 MANAGED CARE PROGRAMS

In an effort to stem sky-rocketing costs and provide adequate health care, managed care organizations such as *health maintenance organizations* (HMOs) and *preferred provider organizations* (PPOs) were developed.

Employers enter into contractual agreements with managed care organizations to provide health care for their employees. Under HMO coverage, patients choose a *primary care physician* (PCP), who is paid a fixed amount by the HMO to care for that patient for a certain amount of time, regardless of the services rendered. Under PPO coverage, insured individuals choose from a list of preferred providers, and receive maximum coverage under a preferred provider's care.

The organizations offering managed care are constantly trying to provide care at the lowest cost possible by negotiating with healthcare providers who agree to provide care for a predetermined fee for service.

Figure 9.4.a

Pharmacy Benefit Managers (PBMs)

Many employers use *pharmacy benefit managers* (PBMs) to handle their employees' prescription needs. In a continued effort to save money, managed care organizations negotiate with PBMs to provide drugs and medical supplies to employees of private companies. Pharmacies who choose to be affiliated with a PBM follow a predetermined formulary and provide services for negotiated fees. PBMs also strive to provide disease management of chronic conditions such as diabetes, hypertension, and asthma in an effort to stem costs related to these conditions. In addition, PBMs often offered employees incentives to purchase maintenance drugs via mail order to save money.

Workers' Compensation

Workers' compensation is handled at a state level and provides medical care coverage and lost wages due to injury, illness, or death directly related to a person's employment. Employees are obligated to notify their employer promptly after an injury and to seek healthcare from a physician or hospital to whom they're referred. The treating physician, hospital, and pharmacy then bills the workers' compensation program for services rendered.

Obtaining Payment from Third Parties

Whether a patient's coverage is provided by a government program such as Medicare or Medicaid, private insurance, or workers' compensation, the pharmacy needs to be paid accurately and promptly. This requires careful attention to details related to the type of insurance coverage a patient presents to the pharmacy. It's often the duty of the pharm tech to accept, verify, and enter the correct information into the patient's profile. Most pharmacies keep a copy of the front and back of the patient's insurance card on file. In addition to filling the prescription and dispensing the medication, the pharmacy technician is often tasked with completing the request for payment.

A large percentage of insurance claims are filed electronically. The pharmacy uses specialized computer software that links the pharmacy and PBM or insurance company via the Internet.

The pharmacy technician is often responsible for using this electronic system to verify coverage and to check that the pharmacy will be reimbursed for the specific prescription requested. Any problems should be brought to the pharmacist's attention so that it can be rectified before the prescription is dispensed to the patient. There are certain items of information that are required by the insurance company for a prescription to be covered.

This information should be obtained when the patient presents the prescription to be filled. Having the patient's correct and current insurance information is vital to the timely payment for pharmacy services rendered.

The necessary information required for reimbursement is located on the patient's insurance card and includes such information as:

- Patient name
- *Patient code*, which indicates the specific patient covered under the plan, as in the subscriber (01), spouse (02), child (03), and so on
- Insurance company/PBM name
- *Subscriber ID number*, also called the patient, or policy, ID number
- *Group number*, which indicates the patient's employer plan code

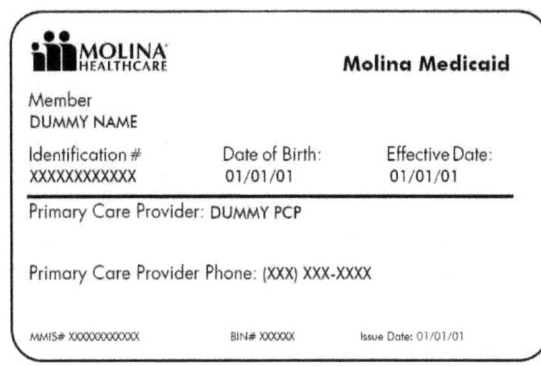

Figure 9.4.b

Additional information, such as bank routing numbers and preauthorization contact information, is located on the back of the patient's insurance card.

In addition to medications and medical supplies, pharmacists are also tasked with providing advice to patients, especially those with chronic conditions such as diabetes, asthma, hypertension, and high cholesterol. Under the *Medicare Modernization Act of 2003*, this counseling is referred to as *medication therapy management services* (MTMS), and pharmacists and other healthcare professionals are allowed to bill and be paid for such services.

Just like other healthcare providers, the pharmacy uses *Current Procedural Terminology (CPT) Codes* to request payment for this care. CPT codes provide very specific explanations of procedures and services provided in a healthcare setting. Select the correct CPT code with care to assure that the claim will be processed promptly.

Incorrect information included on prescription claims will result in an insurance company rejecting the claim.

Medications		Units
Ampicillin, up to 500 mg	J0290	
B-12, up to 1,000 mcg	J3420	
Adrenalin epinephrine inj. 0.1 mg	J0171	
Kenalog, 10 mg	J3301	
Lidocaine, IV, 10 mg	J2001	
Methylprednisolone	J1030	
Methylprednisolone sodium	J2930	
Normal saline, 1000 cc	J7030	
Phenergan, up to 50 mg	J2550	
Progesterone, 1 mg	J1050	
Rocephin, 250 mg	J0696	
Testosterone, 200 mg	J1080	
Tigan, up to 200 mg	J3250	
Toradol, 15 mg	J1885	

Figure 9.4.c

Rejections typically occur because of an error in submitting the request. Coverage will also be denied if there's a lapse of coverage, the refill is requested too early, or the medication requested isn't covered by the plan. Pharmacy technicians are great assets to the pharmacy when they take care to verify current insurance coverage. Accurately filing an insurance claim is the key to prompt payment.

Chapter 9: *Pharmacy Billing and Reimbursement*

Worksheet 9a: Pharmacy Billing and Reimbursement

1. Fill in two (2) similarities and differences for the following terms:
   <u>HMO</u> and <u>PPO</u>

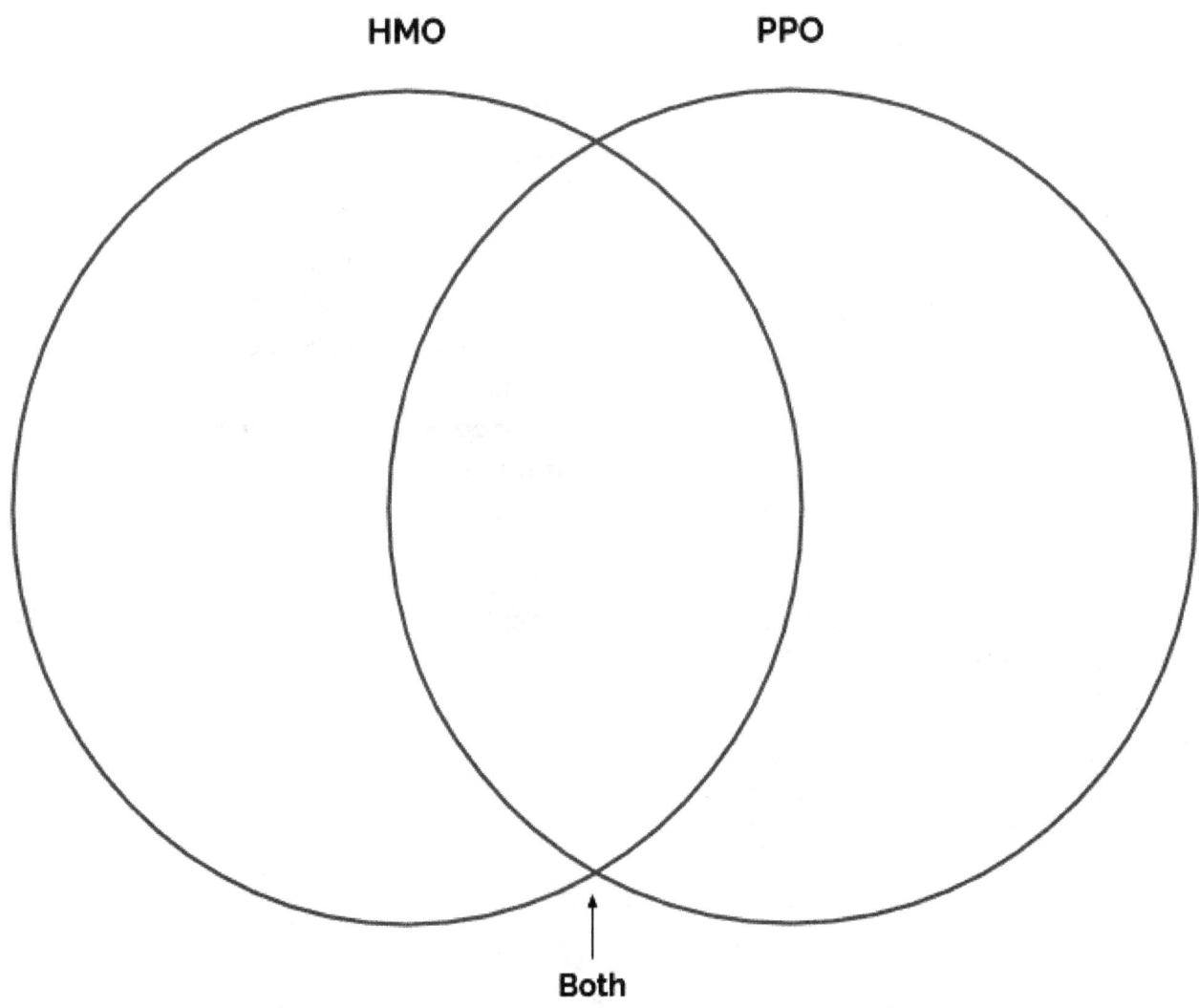

2. What are the three out-of-pocket expenses?

3. Give two examples of durable medical equipment.

Worksheet 9b: Pharmacy Billing and Reimbursement

4. According to the Modernization Act of 2003, the MTMS counseling is a service that can be billed and paid for. True or False?

   True   **False**

5. CPT Codes are utilized in pharmacies like other healthcare services. In what way can CPT Codes encourage the efficiency of claim processing?

   _____

   _____

6. List the two characteristics of both terms below:

Formulary	Open Formulary

7. Which of the following is the full title of MMA?
   a) Medicare Prescription Drug Improvement and Modernization Act
   b) Medicaid Pharmaceutical Drug Improvement and Management Act
   c) Medicare Pharmaceutical Drug Improvement and Management Act
   d) Medicaid Prescription Drug Improvement and Modernization Act

8. The healthcare program for dependents of military personnel in the United States is _____.

Worksheet 9c: Pharmacy Billing and Reimbursement

9. Pharmacies who are affiliated with a PBM follow a predetermined formulary and provide services for negotiated fees. True or false?

    True   **False**

10. Workers' compensation is handled at a _____ level and provides medical care coverage and lost wages due to injury, illness, or death directly related to a person's employment.

    a) Federal
    b) State
    c) Local

Pharmacy Billing & Reimbursement Quiz

1. Which of the following is NOT an example of a claim denial?
   a) Incorrect patient identification number
   b) Incorrect day's supply
   c) Incorrect date of birth
   d) Incorrect label

2. True or False: Prior authorizations may require attention from the provider.

3. Which of the following is NOT a group that administers pharmacy benefits?
   a) DEA
   b) HMO
   c) Medicaid
   d) PPO

4. Which of the following is NOT an example of a plan limitation?
   a) Patient's age
   b) Quantity of medication
   c) Location of refills at a retail or mail order setting
   d) All of the above are examples of plan limitations

5. Coordination of benefits _____.
   a) Helps provide maximum benefits for patients with one insurance provider
   b) Helps provide maximum benefits for patients with more than one insurance provider
   c) Provides patients with an option to purchase another insurance plan
   d) Provides medications to patients at a preset price

6. The part that a customer pays on his or her prescription, after insurance, is called the _____.
   a) Premium
   b) Discount
   c) Co-pay
   d) Coordination of benefits

7. Which of the following is true regarding prior authorizations?
   a) The insurance company will require the prescriber to call the company to validate the necessity of the medication.

b) The patient may have to wait 24-48 hours to receive authorization on a prior authorization request.
c) The prior authorization may be denied and, therefore, the medication will not be covered under insurance
d) All of the above

8. True or False: A worker's compensation claim is billed directly to the patient's worker's compensation plan and not to his or her insurance.

9. The term adjudication means _____.
    a) The process of filling a prescription from beginning to end
    b) Requesting that the prescriber contact the insurance company to validate the medication's necessity
    c) A denial of a prescription claim
    d) The process of paying or denying a claim after it has been submitted to the insurance company

10. True or False: Pharmaceutical companies do not offer prescription assistance programs for selective medications.

Chapter 9: *Pharmacy Billing and Reimbursement*

Quiz: Study Guide

Question Number	Section Reference
1	9.1
2	9.1
3	9.4
4	9.2
5	9.2
6	9.1
7	9.2
8	9.1
9	9.1
10	9.2

Chapter References

Figure 9.1.a: https://images.sampleforms.com/wp-content/uploads/2017/06/New-Patient-Medical-History-Form.jpg

Chart 9.3.a: composed by author

Figure 9.4.a: https://dcs.az.gov/sites/default/files/styles/home_slider/public/CMDP%20Slideshow/cmdp-optumrx-banner-v2.png?itok=54SS8SUZ;
Figure 9.4.b: https://medicaid.ohio.gov/portals/0/Images/MCP/Molina-front.jpg
Figure 9.4.c: https://accesspharmacy.mhmedical.com/data/books/1079/mtm_ch10_f003.png

Chapter 10
Pharmacy Information Systems Usage and Application
Rx Health Academy

General Information

Gone are the days when pharmacy records were kept with pencil and paper. Even though you may receive paper prescription orders, you will be responsible for entering data in the information system used by the pharmacy. Around 10 percent of the questions on the PTCB exam assess knowledge of this area of pharmacy work. Use this study guide to help you prepare for them.

What you'll learn in this chapter

- Pharmacy-related computer applications for documenting the dispensing of prescriptions or medication orders
- Databases, pharmacy computer applications, and documentation management

Chapter Outline

10.1 Computer Applications for Use When Dispensing Prescriptions
10.2 Computer Applications
10.3 Reports
10.4 Standards of Electronic Health Records

Source: Pharmacy Technician Certification Exam (PTCE) Blueprint

Chapter 10: *Pharmacy Information and Systems Usage and Application*

10.1 COMPUTER APPLICATIONS FOR USE WHEN DISPENSING PRESCRIPTIONS

In a community pharmacy, computer programs are used to record patient information and prescription information. It serves as a file of all prescriptions that a patient has received at that pharmacy or pharmacy chain. This file must include all medications dispensed for the last (minimum) 2 years, though many states have stricter laws that must be adhered to.

Electronic Medical Record

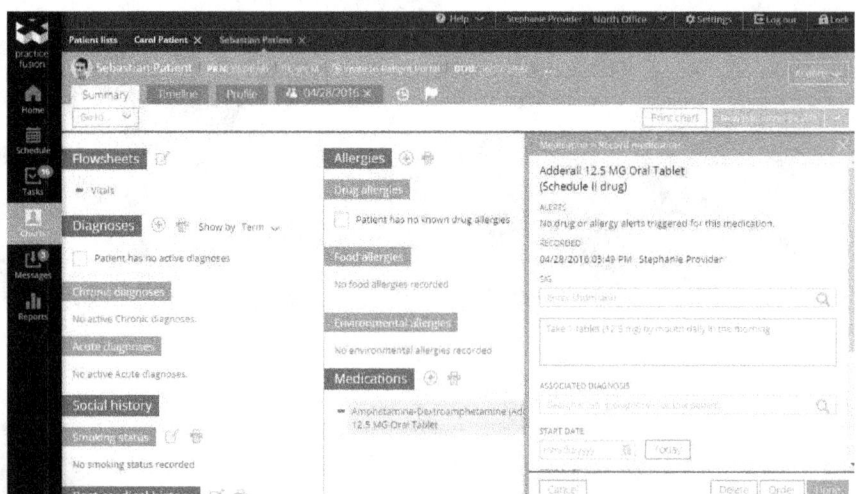

Figure 10.1.a

In a hospital pharmacy, the patient will have an electronic medical record. The medical record will include medical and insurance information, as well as all medications that are ordered by the physician during the patient's stay. When a nurse gives a medication, the time will be recorded in the electronic medical record. The medical record must be maintained even after the patient is discharged. The exact number of years is determined by state law.

Patient Behavior

The electronic profile can be used to track how a patient uses the medication and adheres to instructions. From the profile, pharmacy personnel can see if a patient consistently takes maintenance medication and how often the patient uses his "as needed" medications (PRN).

Other Patient Information

The electronic file will include the patient's name, date of birth, as well as information that is important to know when dispensing a medication. It will include gender, drug allergies, alcohol and/or drug use, and any side effects the patient experienced in the past. The file will also include the patient's location. In a community pharmacy this will be an address, and in a hospital pharmacy this will be a room number and bed number. The patient's profile may include additional information such as a phone number to contact if there is an issue, the name of the

Chapter 10: *Pharmacy Information and Systems Usage and Application*

parent or legal guardian if the patient is a minor, and any medication preference the patient may have.

FDA MedWatch Program

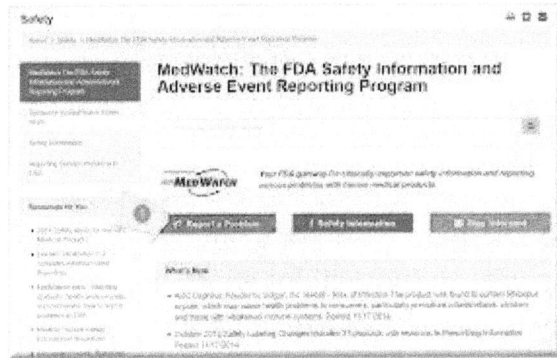

Figure 10.1.b

The FDA has a program called *MedWatch*, where healthcare providers and patients can report an adverse reaction to a medication. A form is filled out electronically. The FDA pays special attention to multiple reports on a single medication and may issue a medication recall if there is a problem. *MedWatch* forms can be accessed at https://www.fda.gov/Safety/MedWatch/.

Medication Dispensing Devices

Some pharmacies have machines to help the pharmacy function efficiently. These machines can include counting machines for pills and tablets, robots that fill and label medication vials, and hospitals commonly have automated dispensing cabinets. These cabinets are known by their trade names *Pyxis*, *Omnicell*, and *MedSelect* and are used to store medication, track inventory of medication, and help ensure patient safety.

Documentation Management

The processing of a prescription is documented at each step and will include an identifier for each person performing that role. Typing a prescription into the computer system, filling the prescription, and verifying the prescriptions are steps that will have the identifier. There may be additional steps, such as the compounding of a prescription, that will be documented as well.

Databases

Pharmacies are required to have access to drug databases. This gives those working in a pharmacy the ability to look up information. As a technician, you may want to look up brand/generic name for unfamiliar medications, whether there is a shortage of a specific medication, in what strengths a medication is available, and how the medication should be stored.

Pharmacoinformatics

Pharmacy computer systems include what is known as *clinical decision support*. The computer will generate an alert for potential medication interactions based on the patient's other medication at that pharmacy. Many times the alert is not significant, but that is a decision the pharmacist will make. As a technician, you will hit "OK" through most of the alerts, but if you notice an alert that looks concerning, notify a senior technician or the pharmacist.

10.2 COMPUTER APPLICATIONS

Figure 10.3.c

Computer applications are used to record and store patient information and medication information. The computer program in a community pharmacy will allow a technician to refill a medication, send insurance information such as a prior authorization to a doctor's office, send refill requests to a doctor's office, and may generate text messages to the patient when the medication is ready for pickup or the patient is due for a refill.

User Access

Each user working in the pharmacy will have a username and a password. The worker will need to sign on at the start of his/her shift and sign out when the shift is finished. The computer program may require additional times of inputting the password, username, or both. The username and password are used to ensure patient privacy, as there is a record of who entered the patient's profile. The username and password serve as a unique identifier and every prescription will have a record of who worked on the prescription, and what they did. The law requires a pharmacy to document who worked on a prescription and what each person did. It is unethical to work using a username or password that is not yours.

Interface

The pharmacy computer system may "interface" or talk to other computer systems. In a hospital pharmacy, the pharmacy computer system may be able to keep track of inventory in an automated dispensing cabinet, and automatically pull up information from the patient's electronic health record or community pharmacy. In a community pharmacy, the system may be able to send refill requests and prior authorization requests directly to doctors' offices.

10.3 REPORTS

Pharmacy software enables a user to generate reports based on data stored on the pharmacy computer. These reports contain objective data, which help identify where improvement is necessary.

Inventory Report

Inventory reports show how much of a certain medication is currently in stock. This report is used to help a pharmacy determine which medications to order and how much of each medication

Chapter 10: *Pharmacy Information and Systems Usage and Application*

should be ordered. Inventory reports are also used to track controlled medication and ensure that diversion is not taking place.

Usage Reports

Usage reports show how many pills of a certain medication are typically used in a defined period of time. These reports are used to anticipate which medications to order and how much should be ordered.

Override Reports

The override report shows many times an override was done in a defined period of time, or how many times a specific user used an override over the last x amount of time. An override report is used to see if the systems in place in a pharmacy are adequate, or if they need adjusting. They are also used to see if members of a pharmacy staff are doing their jobs properly, or if additional training may be necessary.

Diversion Reports

Diversion reports compare the amount of medication inventory that was sent in by the wholesaler with the amount of medication dispensed and the amount currently in stock. This allows the person viewing the report to see if diversion is taking place. Additional reports can then be generated to see when the diversion took place and who was working at that time.

10.4 STANDARDS FOR ELECTRONIC HEALTH RECORDS

Electronic Health Records (EHR) and electronic prescriptions are critical to healthcare. The information contained in these must be able to be securely shared without any fear of hacking or changing the information in any way. The National Council for Prescription Drug Program (NCPDP) establishes technology standards to simplify transferring information between various parties including prescribers, pharmacies, and payers. Here are some of the procedures covered in these standards:

***Financial Information Reporting*—** The NCPDP relays prescription information from the pharmacy to insurance companies for instant billing of prescription information. The pharmacy will receive an instant answer whether the insurance company will cover the medication or if the insurance company rejects the claim. The NCPDP establishes standards for how the amount of medication is billed (per pill, mL, mg, etc.).

Learn more about NCPDP's work to speed time to therapy in Specialty Pharmacy.

***Electronic Audit Requests*—** Insurance companies audit pharmacies to make sure that the information being billed is honest and accurate. The NCPDP establishes the standards for insurance companies to audit a pharmacy and will securely relay information from the pharmacy to the insurance company. The NCPDP also established a standard layout for auditors to view multiple prescriptions at the same time.

Figure 10.3..d   **Formulary and Benefits—** The NCPDP system allows insurance companies to communicate information to prescribers and pharmacy personnel regarding what drugs are on the formulary or are preferred by the insurance company. This information is generally seen on a rejection message.

P*rior Authorization Transfers—* The NCPDP system allows information to be exchanged between pharmacies, prescribers, and insurance companies in order to process prior authorization requests.

Codified Prescription Sig Formatting— The NCPDP establishes how a prescription sig is securely computer-coded in the transfer between the prescriber and the pharmacy.

Telecommunications— Pharmacies often use an interactive voice response (IVR) system that allows individuals to interact with a pharmacy's database. Patients can use the IVR system to order refills or request to speak with a pharmacy staff member, and prescribers can leave prescription messages. There are minimum technological standards to which a pharmacy IVR system must adhere to prevent unauthorized access.

Medicaid Subrogation— The NCPDP system allows a secondary insurance to know that they are not the primary insurance, and the bill must be sent to the primary insurance first. Occasionally, this information is incorrect and the patient will need to call the insurance company and inform them that the insurance is primary for that patient.

Connectivity Operating Rules— The NCPDP establishes standards that are designed to prevent any hacking or changing of EHR information or electronic prescriptions. The computer systems used by the prescribers, pharmacies, and insurance companies must adhere to minimum standards that prevent the hacking into, or changing of, any information.

SCRIPT— NCPDP uses the SCRIPT system to securely send new electronic prescriptions to the pharmacy. SCRIPT is a method of computer coding the prescription so that it can be sent to the pharmacy's computer without any concern of hacking, or if the prescription being changed from the way it was sent by the prescriber.

Pharmacy Information Systems Usage & Application Quiz

1. What is a clinical decision support alert?
   a) An alert that the ordered medication is currently not in stock at the pharmacy
   b) An alert that the ordered medication is being recalled
   c) An alert that the doctor on the prescription is not authorized to order this medication
   d) An alert that the ordered medication may interact with other medications on the patient's profile

2. The National Council for Prescription Drug Programs (NCPDP) provides standards for the electronic exchange of health information. Which of the following is NOT an example of a standard instituted by the NCPDP?
   a) SCRIPT
   b) Codified sig reporting
   c) Prescriber demographic reporting
   d) Financial information reporting

3. Which of the following is an example of an output tool?
   a) Keyboard
   b) Mouse
   c) Scanner
   d) Monitor

4. Which of the following statements best describes pharmacoinformatics?
   a) The integration of information technology to improve patient health care, including medication-related data and knowledge
   b) The use of information technology to replace a pharmacist's retained knowledge
   c) The integration of information technology to access patient data
   d) Using pharmacy computer systems to process prescriptions

5. The clinical decision support system contains patient parameters used to assist pharmacists in making clinical decisions. Which of the following is NOT an example of a patient parameter used in this system?
   a) Drug-drug interaction
   b) Drug-vitamin interactions
   c) Food-food interactions
   d) IV incompatibilities

6. An interface provides a boundary by which information is shared between what two components used in pharmacy information systems?
    a) Printers
    b) Scanners
    c) Computers
    d) Software

7. In which of these scenarios would you report information to the FDA *MedWatch* website?
    a) A patient requests a refill too soon
    b) A patient reports an unusual or dangerous side effect from a medication
    c) A patient brings you a prescription that appears forged

8. What type of information can be saved in a patient's electronic health record (EHR)?
    a) Medical history
    b) Billing information
    c) Allergies
    d) All of the above

9. The pharmacy manager notices that a number of alprazolam tablets are missing. Which of these reports can be used to determine if a pharmacy worker is taking the tablets for personal use?
    a) An inventory report
    b) A usage report
    c) A diversion report

10. Which of these is not a benefit of using an automated dispensing cabinet such as Pyxis, Omnicell, and MedSelect?
    a) Increased patient safety
    b) Secure storage for medication
    c) Automatic ordering of medication

Chapter 10: *Pharmacy Information and Systems Usage and Application*

Quiz: Study Guide

Question Number	Section Reference
1	10.1
2	10.4
3	10.1
4	10.1
5	10.1
6	4.2
7	10.1
8	10.4
9	10.3
10	10.1

Chapter References

Figure 10.1.a: https://www.practicefusion.com/e-prescribing/

Figure 10.2.b: https://www.google.com/search?q=fda+medwatch+program&rlz=1C5CHFA_enUS773US774&source=lnms&tbm=isch&sa=X&ved=0ahUKEwjxmrShk-fjAhXts1kKHb_WBv4Q_AUIEygD&biw=1064&bih=604

Figure 10.3.c: https://ncpdp.org/home

Figure 10.3..d https://www.hfmmagazine.com/articles/2345-five-pharmacy-automation-trends